MW01128823

The Long Labrador Trail

By Dillon Wallace

The Long Labrador Trail

Layout and Cover Copyright ©2010
All Rights Reserved
Printed in the USA
Published by ReadaClassic.com

Table of Contents

TO THE
MEMORY OF MY WIFE

A drear and desolate shore!
Where no tree unfolds its leaves,
And never the spring wind weaves
Green grass for the hunter's tread;
A land forsaken and dead,
Where the ghostly icebergs go
And come with the ebb and flow...

Whittier's "The Rock-tomb of Bradore."

PREFACE

In the summer of 1903 when Leonidas Hubbard, Jr., went to Labrador to explore a section of the unknown interior it was my privilege to accompany him as his companion and friend. The world has heard of the disastrous ending of our little expedition, and how Hubbard, fighting bravely and heroically to the last, finally succumbed to starvation.

Before his death I gave him my promise that should I survive I would write and publish the story of the journey. In "The Lure of The Labrador Wild" that pledge was kept to the best of my ability.

While Hubbard and I were struggling inland over those desolate wastes, where life was always uncertain, we entered into a compact that in case one of us fall the other would carry to completion the exploratory work that he had planned and begun. Providence willed that it should become my duty to fulfill this compact, and the following pages are a record of how it was done.

Not I, but Hubbard, planned the journey of which this book tells, and from him I received the inspiration and with him the training and experience that enabled me to succeed. It was his spirit that led me on over the wearisome trails, and through the rushing rapids, and to him and to his memory belong the credit and the honor of success.

D. W. February, 1907.

Chapter 1: The Voice of the Wilderness

"It's always the way, Wallace! When a fellow starts on the long trail, he's never willing to quit. It'll be the same with you if you go with me to Labrador. When you come home, you'll hear the voice of the wilderness calling you to return, and it will lure you back again."

It seems but yesterday that Hubbard uttered those prophetic words as he and I lay before our blazing camp fire in the snow-covered Shawangunk Mountains on that November night in the year 1901, and planned that fateful trip into the unexplored Labrador wilderness which was to cost my dear friend his life, and both of us indescribable sufferings and hardships. And how true a prophecy it was! You who have smelled the camp fire smoke; who have drunk in the pure forest air, laden with the smell of the fir tree; who have dipped your paddle into untamed waters, or climbed mountains, with the knowledge that none but the red man has been there before you; or have, perchance, had to fight the wilds and nature for your very existence; you of the wilderness brotherhood can understand how the fever of exploration gets into one's blood and draws one back again to the forests and the barrens in spite of resolutions to "go no more."

It was more than this, however, that lured me back to Labrador. There was the vision of dear old Hubbard as I so often saw him during our struggle through that rugged northland wilderness, wasted in form and ragged in dress, but always hopeful and eager, his undying spirit and indomitable will focused in his words to me, and I can still see him as he looked when he said them:

"The work must be done, Wallace, and if one of us falls before it is completed the other must finish it."

I went back to Labrador to do the work he had undertaken, but which he was not permitted to accomplish. His exhortation appealed to me as a command from my leader--a call to duty.

Hubbard had planned to penetrate the Labrador peninsula from Groswater Bay, following the old northern trail of the Mountaineer Indians from Northwest River Post of the Hudson's Bay Company, situated on Groswater Bay, one hundred and forty miles inland from the eastern coast, to Lake Michikamau, thence through the lake and northward over the divide, where he hoped to locate the headwaters of the George River.

It was his intention to pass down this river until he reached the hunting camps of the Nenenot or Nascaupee Indians, there witness the annual migration of the caribou to the eastern seacoast, which tradition said took place about the middle or latter part of September, and to be present at the "killing," when the Indians, it was reported, secured their winter's supply of provisions by spearing the caribou while the herds were swimming the river. The caribou hunt over, he was to have returned across country to the St. Lawrence or retrace his steps to Northwest River Post, whichever might seem advisable. Should the season, however, be too far advanced to permit of a safe return, he was to have proceeded down the river to its mouth, at Ungava Bay, and return to civilization in winter with dogs.

The country through which we were to have traveled was to be mapped so far as possible, and observations made of the geological formation and of the flora, and as many specimens collected as possible.

This, then, Hubbard's plan, was the plan which I adopted and which I set out to accomplish, when, in March, 1905, I finally decided to return to Labrador.

It was advisable to reach Hamilton Inlet with the opening of navigation and make an early start into the country, for every possible day of the brief summer would be needed for our purpose.

It was, as I fully realized, no small undertaking. Many hundreds of miles of unknown country must be traversed, and over mountains and through marshes for long distances our

9

canoes and outfit would have to be transported upon the backs of the men comprising my party, as pack animals cannot be used in Labrador.

Through immense stretches of country there would be no sustenance for them, and, in addition to this, the character of the country itself forbids their use.

The personnel of the expedition required much thought. I might with one canoe and one or two professional Indian packers travel more rapidly than with men unused to exploration work, but in that case scientific research would have to be slighted. I therefore decided to sacrifice speed to thoroughness and to take with me men who, even though they might not be physically able to carry the large packs of the professional voyageur, would in other respects lend valuable assistance to the work in hand.

My projected return to Labrador was no sooner announced than numerous applications came to me from young men anxious to join the expedition. After careful investigation, I finally selected as my companions George M. Richards, of Columbia University, as geologist and to aid me in the topographical work, Clifford H. Easton, who had been a student in the School of Forestry at Biltmore, North Carolina (both residents of New York), and Leigh Stanton, of Halifax, Nova Scotia, a veteran of the Boer War, whom I had met at the lumber camps in Groswater Bay, Labrador, in the winter of 1903-1904, when he was installing the electric light plant in the large lumber mill there.

It was desirable to have at least one Indian in the party as woodsman, hunter and general camp servant. For this position my friend, Frank H. Keefer, of Port Arthur, Ontario, recommended to me, and at my request engaged, Peter Stevens, a full-blood Ojibway Indian, of Grand Marais, Minnesota. "Pete" arrived in New York under the wing of the railway conductor during the last week in May.

In the meantime I had devoted myself to the selection and purchase of our instruments and general outfit. Everything must be purchased in advance--from canoes to repair kit--as my former experience in Labrador had taught me. It may be of interest to mention the most important items of outfit and the food supply with which we were provided: Two canvas-covered canoes, one nineteen and one eighteen feet in length; one seven by nine "A" tent, made of waterproof "balloon" silk; one tarpaulin, seven by nine feet; folding tent stove and pipe; two tracking lines; three small axes; cooking outfit, consisting of two frying pans, one mixing pan and three aluminum kettles; an aluminum plate, cup and spoon for each man; one .33 caliber high-power Winchester rifle and two 44-40 Winchester carbines (only one of these carbines was taken with us from New York, and this was intended as a reserve gun in case the party should separate and return by different routes. The other was one used by Stanton when previously in Labrador, and taken by him in addition to the regular outfit). One double barrel 12-gauge shotgun; two ten-inch barrel single shot .22 caliber pistols for partridges and small game; ammunition; tumplines; three fishing rods and tackle, including trolling outfits; one three and one-half inch gill net; repair kit, including necessary material for patching canoes, clothing, etc.; matches, and a medicine kit.

The following instruments were also carried: Three minimum registering thermometers; one aneroid barometer which was tested and set for me by the United States Weather Bureau; one clinometer; one pocket transit; three compasses; one pedometer; one taffrail log; one pair binoculars; three No. 3A folding pocket Kodaks, sixty rolls of films, each roll sealed in a tin can and waterproofed, and six "Vanguard" watches mounted in dust-proof cases.

Each man was provided with a sheath knife and a waterproof match box, and his personal kit, containing a pair of blankets and clothing, was carried in a waterproof canvas bag.

I may say here in reference to these waterproof bags and the "balloon" silk tent that they were of the same manufacture as those used on the Hubbard expedition and for their purpose as nearly perfect as it is possible to make them. The tent weighed but nine pounds, was windproof, and, like the bags, absolutely waterproof, and the, material strong and firm.

Our provision supply consisted of 298 pounds of pork; 300 pounds of flour; 45 pounds of corn meal; 40 pounds of lentils; 28 pounds of rice; 25 pounds of erbswurst; 10 pounds of prunes; a few packages of dried vegetables; some beef bouillon tablets; 6 pounds of baking powder; 16 pounds of tea; 6 pounds of coffee; 15 pounds of sugar; 14 pounds of salt; a small amount of saccharin and crystallose, and 150 pounds of pemmican.

Everything likely to be injured by water was packed in waterproof canvas bags.

My friend Dr. Frederick A. Cook, of the Arctic Club, selected my medical kit, and instructed me in the use of its simple remedies. It was also upon the recommendation of Dr. Cook and others of my Arctic Club friends that I purchased the pemmican, which was designed as an emergency ration, and it is worth noting that one pound of pemmican, as our experience demonstrated, was equal to two or even three pounds of any other food that we carried. Its ingredients are ground dried beef, tallow, sugar, raisins and currants.

We had planned to go north from St. Johns on the Labrador mail boat Virginia Lake, which, as I had been informed by the Reid- Newfoundland Company, was expected to sail from St. Johns on her first trip on or about June tenth. This made it necessary for us to leave New York on the Red Cross Line steamer Rosalind sailing from Brooklyn on May thirtieth; and when, at eleven-thirty that Tuesday morning, the Rosalind cast loose from her wharf, we and our outfit were aboard, and our journey of eleven long months was begun.

As I waved farewell to our friends ashore I recalled that other day two years before, when Hubbard and I had stood on the Silvia's deck, and I said to myself:

"Well, this, too, is Hubbard's trip. His spirit is with me. It was he, not I, who planned this Labrador work, and if I succeed it will be because of him and his influence."

I was glad to be away. With every throb of the engine my heart grew lighter. I was not thinking of the perils I was to face with my new companions in that land where Hubbard and I had suffered so much. The young men with me were filled with enthusiasm at the prospect of adventure in the silent and mysterious country for which they were bound.

Chapter 2: On the Threshold of the Unknown

"When shall we reach Rigolet, Captain?"

"Before daylight, I hope, sir, if the fog holds off, but there's a mist settling, and if it gets too thick, we may have to come to."

Crowded with an unusual cargo of humanity, fishermen going to their summer work on "The Labrador" with their accompanying tackle and household goods, meeting with many vexatious delays in discharging the men and goods at the numerous ports of call, and impeded by fog and wind, the mail boat Virginia Lake had been much longer than is her wont on her trip "down north."

It was now June twenty-first. Six days before (June fifteenth), when we boarded the ship at St. Johns we had been informed that the steamer Harlow, with a cargo for the lumber mills at Kenemish, in Groswater Bay, was to leave Halifax that very afternoon. She could save us a long and disagreeable trip in an open boat, ninety miles up Groswater Bay, and I bad hoped that we might reach Rigolet in time to secure a passage for myself and party from that point. But the Harlow had no ports of call to make, and it was predicted that her passage from Halifax to Rigolet would be made in four days.

I had no hope now of reaching Rigolet before her, or of finding her there, and, resigned to my fate, I left the captain on the bridge and went below to my stateroom to rest until daylight. Sometime in the night I was aroused by someone saying:

"We're at Rigolet, sir, and there's a ship at anchor close by."

Whether I had been asleep or not, I was fully awake now, and found that the captain had come to tell me of our arrival. The fog had held off and we had done much better than the captain's prediction. Hurrying into my clothes, I went on deck, from which, through the slight haze that hung over the water, I could discern the lights of a ship, and beyond, dimly visible, the old familiar line of Post buildings showing against the dark spruce-covered hills behind, where the great silent forest begins.

All was quiet save for the thud, thud, thud of the oarlocks of a small boat approaching our ship and the dismal howl of a solitary "husky" dog somewhere ashore. The captain had preceded me on deck, and in answer to my inquiries as to her identity said he did not know whether the stranger at anchor was the Harlow or not, but he thought it was.

We had to wait but a moment, however, for the information. The small boat was already alongside, and John Groves, a Goose Bay trader and one of my friends of two years before, clambered aboard and had me by the hand.

"I'm glad to see you, sir; and how is you?"

Assuring him that I was quite well, I asked the name of the other ship.

"The Harlow, sir, an' she's goin' to Kenemish with daylight."

"Well, I must get aboard of her then, and try to get a passage up. Is your flat free, John, to take me aboard of her?"

"Yes, sir. Step right in, sir. But I thinks you'd better go ashore, for the Harlow's purser's ashore. If you can't get passage on the Harlow my schooner's here doing nothin' while I goes to St. Johns for goods, and I'll have my men run you up to Nor'west River."

I thanked him and lost no time in going ashore in his boat, where I found Mr. James Fraser, the factor, and received a hearty welcome. In Mr. Fraser's office I found also the purser of the Harlow, and I quickly arranged with him for a passage to Kenemish, which is ninety miles up the inlet, and just across Groswater Bay (twelve miles) from Northwest River Post. The Harlow was to sail at daylight and I at once returned to the mail boat, called the boys and, with the help of the Virginia's crew and one of their small boats, we were transferred, bag and baggage, to the Harlow.

Owing to customs complications the Harlow was later than expected in leaving Rigolet, and it was evening before she dropped anchor at Kenemish. I went ashore in the ship's boat and visited again the lumber camp "cook house" where Dr. Hardy and I lay ill throng those weary winter weeks, and where poor Hardy died. Hardy was the young lumber company doctor who treated my frozen feet in the winter of 1903-1904. Here I met Fred Blake, a Northwest River trapper. Fred had his flat, and I engaged him to take a part of our luggage to Northwest River. Then I returned to the ship to send the boys ahead with the canoes and some of our baggage, while I waited behind to follow with Fred and the rest of the kit in his flat a half hour later.

Fred and I were hardly a mile from the ship when a heavy thunderstorm broke upon us, and we were soon drenching wet--the baptism of our expedition. This rain was followed by a dense fog and early darkness. On and on we rowed, and I was berating myself for permitting the men to go on so far ahead of us with the canoes, for they did not know the way and the fog had completely shut out the lights of the Post buildings, which otherwise would have been visible across the bay for a considerable distance.

Suddenly through the fog and darkness, from shoreward, came a "Hello! Hello!" We answered, and heading our boat toward the sound of continued "Hellos," found the men, with the canoes unloaded and hauled ashore, preparing to make a night camp. I joined them and, launching and reloading the canoes again, with Richards and Easton in one canoe and Pete and I in the other, we followed Fred and Stanton, who preceded us in the rowboat, keeping our canoes religiously within earshot of Fred's thumping oarlocks. Finally the fog lifted, and not far away we caught a glimmer of lights at the French Post. All was dark at the Hudson Bay Post across the river when at last our canoes touched the sandy beach and we sprang ashore.

What a flood of remembrances came to me as I stepped again upon the old familiar ground! How vividly I remembered that June day when Hubbard and I had first set foot on this very ground and Mackenzie had greeted us so cordially! And also that other day in November when, ragged and starved, I came here to tell of Hubbard, lying dead in the dark forest beyond! The same dogs that I had known then came running to meet us now, the faithful fellows with which I began that sad funeral journey homeward over the ice. I called some of them by name "Kumalik," "Bo'sun," "Captain," "Tinker"--and they pushed their great heads against my legs and, I believe, recognized me.

It was nearly two o'clock in the morning. We went immediately to the Post house and roused out Mr. Stuart Cotter, the agent (Mackenzie is no longer there), and received from him a royal welcome. He called his Post servant and instructed him to bring in our things, and while we changed our dripping clothes for dry ones, his housekeeper prepared a light supper. It was five o'clock in the morning when I retired.

In the previous autumn I had written Duncan McLean, one of the four men who came to my rescue on the Susan River, that should I ever come to Labrador again and be in need of a man I would like to engage him. Cotter told me that Duncan had just come from his trapping path and was at the Post kitchen, so when we had finished breakfast, at eight o'clock that morning, I saw Duncan and, as he was quite willing to go with us, I arranged with him to accompany us a short distance into the country to help us pack over the first portage and to bring back letters.

He expressed a wish to visit his father at Kenemish before starting into the country, but promised to be back the next evening ready for the start on Monday morning, the twenty-sixth, and I consented. I knew hard work was before us, and as I wished all hands to be well rested and fresh at the outset, I felt that a couple of days' idleness would do us no harm.

Some five hundred yards east of Mr. Cotter's house is an old, abandoned mission chapel, and behind it an Indian burying ground. The cleared space of level ground between the house and chapel was, for a century or more, the camping ground of the Mountaineer Indians who come to the Post each spring to barter or sell their furs. In the olden time there were nearly a hundred families of them, whose hunting ground was that section of country between Hamilton Inlet and the Upper George River.

These people now, for the most part, hunt south of the inlet and trade at the St. Lawrence Posts. The chapel was erected about 1872, but ten years ago the Jesuit missionary was withdrawn, and since then the building has fallen into decay and ruin, and the crosses that marked the graves in the old burying grounds have been broken down by the heavy winter snows. It was this withdrawal of the missionary that turned the Indians to the southward, where priests are more easily found. The Mountaineer Indian, unlike the Nascaupee, is very religious, and must, at least once a year, meet his father confessor. The camping ground since the abandonment of the mission, has lain lonely and deserted, save for three or four families who, occasionally in the summer season, come back again to pitch their tents where their forefathers camped and held their annual feasts in the old days.

Competition between the trading companies at this point has raised the price of furs to such an extent that the few families of Indians that trade at this Post are well-to-do and very independent. There were two tents of them here when we arrived--five men and several women and children. I found two of my old friends there--John and William Ahsini. They expressed pleasure in meeting me again, and a lively interest in our trip. With Mr. Cotter acting as interpreter, John made for me a map of the old Indian trail from Grand Lake to Seal Lake, and William a map to Lake Michikamau and over the height of land to the George River, indicating the portages and principal intervening lakes as they remembered them.

Seal Lake is a large lake expansion of the Nascaupee River, which river, it should be explained, is the outlet of Lake Michikamau and discharges its waters into Grand Lake and through Grand Lake into Groswater Bay. Lake Michikamau, next to Lake Mistasinni, is the largest lake in the Labrador peninsula, and approximately from eighty to ninety miles in length. Neither John nor William had been to Lake Michikamau by this route since they were young lads, but they told us that the Indians, when traveling very light without their families, used to make the journey in twenty-three days.

During my previous stay in Labrador one Indian told me it could be done in ten days, while another said that Indians traveling very fast would require about thirty days. It is difficult to base calculations upon information of this kind. But I was sure that, with our comparatively heavy outfit, and the fact that we would have to find the trail for ourselves, we should require at least twice the time of the Indians, who know every foot of the way as we know our familiar city streets at home.

They expressed their belief that the old trail could be easily found, and assured us that each portage, as we asked about it in detail, was a "miam potagan" (good portage), but at the same time expressed their doubts as to our ability to cross the country safely.

In fact, it has always been the Indians' boast, and I have heard it many times, that no white man could go from Groswater Bay to Ungava alive without Indians to help him through. "Pete" was a Lake Superior Indian and had never run a rapid in his life. He was to spend the night with Tom Blake and his family in their snug little log cabin, and be ready for an early start up Grand Lake on the morrow. It was Tom that headed the little party sent by me up the Susan Valley to bring to the Post Hubbard's body in March, 1904; and it was through his perseverance, loyalty and hard work at the time that I finally succeeded in recovering the body. Tom's daughter, Lillie, was Mackenzie's little housekeeper, who showed me so many kindnesses then. The whole family, in fact, were very good to me during those trying days, and I count them among my true and loyal friends.

We had supper with Cotter, who sang some Hudson's Bay songs, Richards sang a jolly college song or two, Stanton a "classic," and then all who could sing joined in "Auld Lang Syne."

My thoughts were of that other day, when Hubbard, so full of hope, had begun this same journey-of the sunshine and fleecy clouds and beckoning fir tops, and I wondered what was in store for us now.

Chapter 3: The Last of Civilization

The time for action had come. Our canoes were loaded near the wharf, we said good-by to Cotter and a group of native trapper friends, and as we took our places in the canoes and dipped our paddles into the waters that were to carry us northward the Post flag was run up on the flagpole as a salute and farewell, and we were away. We soon rounded the point, and Cotter and the trappers and the Post were lost to view. Duncan was to follow later in the evening in his rowboat with some of our outfit which we left in his charge.

Silently we paddled through the "little lake." The clouds hung somber and dull with threatening rain, and a gentle breeze wafted to us now and again a bit of fragrance from the spruce-covered hills above us. Almost before I realized it we were at the rapid. Away to the westward stretched Grand Lake, deep and dark and still, with the rugged outline of Cape Corbeau in the distance.

Tom Blake and his family, one and all, came out to give us the whole- souled, hospitable welcome of "The Labrador." Even Atikamish, the little Indian dog that Mackenzie used to have, but which he had given to Tom when he left Northwest River, was on hand to tell me in his dog language that he remembered me and was delighted to see me back. Here we would stay for the night--the last night for months that we were to sleep in a habitation of civilized man.

The house was a very comfortable little log dwelling containing a small kitchen, a larger living-room which also served as a sleeping- room, and an attic which was the boys' bedroom. The house was comfortably furnished, everything clean to perfection, and the atmosphere of love and home that dwelt here was long remembered by us while we huddled in many a dreary camp during the weeks that followed.

Duncan did not come that night, and it was not until ten o'clock the next morning (June twenty-seventh) that he appeared. Then we made ready for the start. Tom and his young son Henry announced their intention of accompanying us a short distance up Grand Lake in their small sailboat. Mrs. Blake gave us enough bread and buns, which she had baked especially for us, to last two or three days, and she gave us also a few fresh eggs, saying, "'Twill be a long time before you has eggs again."

At half-past ten o'clock our canoes were afloat, farewell was said, and we were beyond the last fringe of civilization.

The morning was depressing and the sky was overcast with low-hanging, heavy clouds, but almost with our start, as if to give us courage for our work and fire our blood, the leaden curtain was drawn aside and the deep blue dome of heaven rose above us. The sun shone warm and bright, and the smell of the fresh damp forest, the incense of the wilderness gods, was carried to us by a puff of wind from the south which enabled Duncan to hoist his sails. The rest of us bent to our paddles, and all were eager to plunge into the unknown and solve the mystery of what lay beyond the horizon.

Our nineteen-foot canoe was manned by Pete in the bow, Stanton in the center and Easton in the stern, while I had the bow and Richards the stern of the eighteen-foot canoe. We paddled along the north shore of the lake, close to land. Stanton, with an eye for fresh meat, espied a porcupine near the water's edge and stopped to kill it, thus gaining the honor of having bagged the first game of the trip. At twelve o'clock we halted for luncheon, in almost the same spot where Hubbard and I had lunched when going up Grand Lake two years before. While Pete cooked bacon and eggs and made tea, Stanton and Richards dressed the porcupine for supper.

After luncheon we cut diagonally across the lake to the southern shore, passed Cape Corbeau River and landed near the base of Cape Corbeau bluff, that the elevation might be taken and geological specimens secured. After making our observations we turned again toward the northern shore, where more specimens were collected. Here Tom and Henry Blake said goodbye to us and turned homeward.

During the afternoon Stanton and I each killed a porcupine, making three in all for the day--a good beginning in the matter of game.

At sunset we landed at Watty's Brook, a small stream flowing into Grand Lake from the north, and some twenty miles above the rapid. Our progress during the day had been slow, as the wind had died away and we had, several times, to wait for Duncan to overtake us in his slower rowboat.

While the rest of us "made camp" Duncan cut wood for a rousing fire, as the evening was cool, and Pete put a porcupine to boil for supper. We were a hungry crowd when we sat down to eat. I had told the boys how good porcupine was, how it resembled lamb and what a treat we were to have. But all porcupines are not alike, and this one was not within my reckoning. Tough! He was certainly "the oldest inhabitant," and after vain efforts to chew the leathery meat, we turned in disgust to bread and coffee, and Easton, at least, lost faith forever in my judgment of toothsome game, and formed a particular prejudice against porcupines which he never overcame. Pete assured us, however, that, "This porcupine, he must boil long. I boil him again to-night and boil him again to-morrow morning. Then he very good for breakfast. Porcupine fine. Old one must be cooked long."

So Pete, after supper, put the porcupine on to cook some more, promising that we should find it nice and tender for breakfast.

As I sat that night by the low-burning embers of our first camp fire I forgot my new companions. Through the gathering night mists I could just discern the dim outlines of the opposite shore of Grand Lake. It was over there, just west of that high spectral bluff, that Hubbard and I, on a wet July night, had pitched our first camp of the other trip. In fancy I was back again in that camp and Hubbard was talking to me and telling me of the "bully story" of the mystic land of wonders that lay "behind the ranges" he would have to take back to the world.

"We're going to traverse a section no white man has ever seen," he exclaimed, "and we'll add something to the world's knowledge of geography at least, and that's worthwhile. No matter how little a man may add to the fund of human knowledge it's worth the doing, for it's by little bits that we've learned to know so much of our old world. There's some hard work before us, though, up there in those hills, and some hardships to meet."

Ah, if we had only known!

Someone said it was time to "turn in," and I was brought suddenly to a sense of the present, but a feeling of sadness possessed me when I took my place in the crowded tent, and I lay awake long, thinking of those other days.

Clear and crisp was the morning of June twenty-eighth. The atmosphere was bracing and delightful, the azure of the sky above us shaded to the most delicate tints of blue at the horizon, and, here and there, bits of clouds, like bunches of cotton, flecked the sky. The sun broke grandly over the rugged hills, and the lake, like molten silver, lay before us.

A fringe of ice had formed during the night along the shore. We broke it and bathed our hands and faces in the cool water, then sat down in a circle near our camp fire to renew our attack upon the porcupine, which had been sending out a most delicious odor from the kettle where Pete had it cooking. But alas for our expectations! Our teeth would make no impression upon it, and Easton remarked that "the rubber trust ought to hunt porcupines, for they are a lot tougher than rubber and just as pliable."

"I don't know why," said Pete sadly. "I boil him long time."

That day we continued our course along the northern shore of the lake until we reached the deep bay which Hubbard and I had failed to enter and explore on the other trip, and which failure had resulted so tragically. This bay is some five miles from the westerly end of Grand Lake, and is really the mouth of the Nascaupee and Crooked Rivers which flow into the upper end of it. There was little or no wind and we had to go slowly to permit Duncan, in his rowboat, to keep pace with us. Darkness was not far off when we reached Duncan's tilt (a small log hut), three miles up the Nascaupee River, where we stopped for the night.

This is the tilt in which Allen Goudy and Duncan lived at the time they came to my rescue in 1903, and where I spent three days getting strength for my trip down Grand Lake to the Post.

It is Duncan's sup- ply base in the winter months when he hunts along the Nascaupee River, one hundred and twenty miles inland to Seal Lake. On this hunting "path" Duncan has two hundred and fifty marten and forty fox traps, and, in the spring, a few bear traps besides.

The country has been burned here. Just below Duncan's tilt is a spruce-covered island, but the mainland has a stunted new growth of spruce, with a few white birch, covering the wreck of the primeval forest that was flame swept thirty odd years ago. Over some considerable areas no new growth to speak of has appeared, and the charred remains of the dead trees stand stark and gray, or lie about in confusion upon the ground, giving the country a particularly dreary and desolate appearance.

The morning of June twenty-ninth was overcast and threatened rain, but toward evening the sky cleared.

Progress was slow, for the current in the river here was very strong, and paddling or rowing against it was not easy. We had to stop several times and wait for Duncan to overtake us with his boat. Once he halted to look at a trap where he told us he had caught six black bears. It was nearly sunset when we reached the mouth of the Red River, nineteen miles above Grand Lake, where it flows into the Nascaupee from the west. This is a wide, shallow stream whose red- brown waters were quite in contrast to the clear waters of the Nascaupee.

Opposite the mouth of the Red River, and on the eastern shore of the Nascaupee, is the point where the old Indian trail was said to begin, and on a knoll some fifty feet above the river we saw the wigwam poles of an old Indian camp, and a solitary grave with a rough fence around it. Here we landed and awaited Duncan, who had stopped at another of his trapping tilts three or four hundred yards below. When he joined us a little later, in answer to my inquiry as to whether this was the beginning of the old trail, he answered, "'Tis where they says the Indians came out, and some of the Indians has told me so. I supposes it's the place, sir."

"But have you never hunted here yourself?" I asked.

"No, sir, I've never been in here at all. I travels right past up the Nascaupee. All I knows about it, sir, is what they tells me. I always follows the Nascaupee, sir."

23

Above us rose a high, steep hill covered for two-thirds of the way from its base with a thick growth of underbrush, but quite barren on top save for a few bunches of spruce brush.

The old trail, unused for eight or ten years, headed toward the hill and was quite easily traced for some fifty yards from the old camp. Then it disappeared completely in a dense undergrowth of willows, alders and spruce.

While Pete made preparation for our supper and Duncan unloaded his boat and hauled it up preparatory to leaving it until his return from the interior, the rest of us tried to follow the trail through the brush. But beyond where the thick undergrowth began there was nothing at all that, to us, resembled a trail. Finally, I instructed Pete to go with Richards and see what he could do while the rest of us made camp. Pete started ahead, forging his way through the thick growth. In ten minutes I heard him shout from the hillside, "He here--I find him," and saw Pete hurrying up the steep incline.

When Richards and Pete returned an hour later we had camp pitched and supper cooking. They reported the trail, as far as they had gone, very rough and hard to find. For some distance it would have to be cut out with an ax, and nowhere was it bigger than a rabbit run. Duncan rather favored going as far, as Seal Lake by the trail that he knew and which followed the Nascaupee. This trail he believed to be much easier than the long unused Indian trail, which was undoubtedly in many places entirely obscured and in any case extremely difficult to follow. I dismissed his suggestion, however, with little consideration. My, object was to trace the old Indian trail and explore as much of the country as possible, and not to hide myself in an enclosed river valley. Therefore, I decided that next day we should scout ahead to the first water to which the trail led and cut out the trail where necessary. The work I knew would be hard, but we were expecting to do hard work. We were not on a summer picnic.

A rabbit which Stanton had shot and a spruce grouse that fell before Pete's pistol, together with what remained of our porcupine, hot coffee, and Mrs. Blake's good bread, made a supper that we ate with zest while we talked over the prospects of the trail. Supper finished, Pete carefully washed his dishes, then carefully washed his dishcloth, which latter he hung upon a bough near the fire to dry. His cleanliness about his cooking was a revelation to me. I had never before seen a camp man or guide so neat in this respect.

The real work of the trip was now to begin, the hard portaging, the trail finding and trail making, and we were to break the seal of a land that had, through the ages, held its secret from all the world, excepting the red man. This is what we were thinking of when we gathered around our camp fire that evening, and filled and lighted our pipes and puffed silently while we watched the newborn stars of evening come into being one by one until the arch of heaven was aglow with the splendor of a Labrador night. And when we at length went to our bed of spruce boughs it was to dream of strange scenes and new worlds that we were to conquer.

Chapter 4: On the Old Indian Trail

Next morning we scouted ahead and found that the trail led to a small lake some five and a half miles beyond our camp. For a mile or so the brush was pretty thick and the trail was difficult to follow, but beyond that it was comparatively well defined though exceedingly steep, the hill rising to an elevation of one thousand and fifty feet above the Nascaupee River in the first two miles. We had fifteen hundred pounds of outfit to carry upon our backs, and I realized that at first we should have to trail slowly and make several loads of it, for, with the exception of Pete, none of the men was in training. The work was totally different from anything to which they had been accustomed, and as I did not wish to break their spirits or their ardor, I instructed them to carry only such packs as they could walk under with perfect ease until they should become hardened to the work.

The weather had been cool and bracing, but as if to add to our difficulties the sun now boiled down, and the black flies-- "the devil's angels" someone called them, came in thousands to feast upon the newcomers and make life miserable for us all. Duncan was as badly treated by them as any of us, although he belonged to the country, and I overheard him swearing at a lively gait soon after the little beasts began their attacks.

"Why, Duncan," said I, "I didn't know you swore."

"I does, sir, sometimes--when things makes me," he replied.

"But it doesn't help matters any to swear, does it?"

"No, sir, but" (swatting his face) "damn the flies--it's easin' to the feelin's to swear sometimes."

On several occasions after this, I heard Duncan "easin' his

feelin's" in long and astounding bursts of profane eloquence, but he did try to moderate his language when I was within earshot. Once I asked him:

"Where in the world did you learn to swear like that, Duncan?"

"At the lumber camps, sir," he replied.

In the year I had spent in Labrador I had never before heard a planter or native of Groswater Bay swear. But this explained it. The lumbermen from "civilization" were educating them.

At one o'clock on July first, half our outfit was portaged to the summit of the hill and we ate our dinner there in the broiling sun, for we were above the trees, which ended some distance below us. It was fearfully hot--a dead, suffocating heat--with not a breath of wind to relieve the stifling atmosphere, and someone asked what the temperature was.

"Eighty-seven in the shade, but no shade," Richards remarked as he threw down his pack and consulted the thermometer where I had placed it under a low bush. "I'll swear it's a hundred and fifty in the sun."

During dinner Pete pointed to the river far below us, saying, "Look! Indian canoe." I could not make it out without my binoculars, but with their aid discerned a canoe on the river, containing a solitary paddler. None of us, excepting Pete, could see the canoe without the glasses, at which he was very proud and remarked: "No findin' glass need me. See far, me. See long way off."

On other occasions, afterward, I had reason to marvel at Pete's clearness of vision.

It was John Ahsini in the canoe, as we discovered later when he joined us and helped Stanton up the hill with his last pack to our night camp on the summit. I invited John to eat supper with us and he accepted the invitation. He told us he was hunting "moshku" (bear) and was camped at the mouth of the Red River. He assured us that we would find no more hills like this one we were on, and, pointing to the northward, said, "Miam potagan" (good portage) and that we would find plenty "atuk" (caribou), "moshku" and "mashumekush" (trout). After supper I gave John some "stemmo," and he disappeared down the trail to join his wife in their wigwam below.

We were all of us completely exhausted that night. Stanton

27

was too tired to eat, and lay down upon the bare rocks to sleep. Pete stretched our tent wigwam fashion on some old Indian tepee poles, and, without troubling ourselves to break brush for a bed, we all soon joined Stanton in a dreamless slumber upon his rocky couch.

The night, like the day, was very warm, and when I aroused Pete at sunrise the next morning (July second) to get breakfast the mosquitoes were about our heads in clouds.

A magnificent panorama lay before us. Opposite, across the valley of the Nascaupee, a great hill held its snow-tipped head high in the heavens. Some four miles farther up to the northwest, the river itself, where it was choked with blocks of ice, made its appearance and threaded its way down to the southeast until it was finally lost in the spruce-covered valley. Beyond, bits of Grand Lake, like silver settings in the black surrounding forest, sparkled in the light of the rising sun. Away to the westward could be traced the rushing waters of the Red River making their course down through the sandy ridges that enclose its valley. To the northward lay a great undulating wilderness, the wilderness that we were to traverse. It was Sunday morning, and the holy stillness of the day engulfed our world.

When Pete had the fire going and the kettle singing I roused the boys and told them we would make this, our first Sunday in the bush, an easy one, and simply move our camp forward to a more hospitable and sheltered spot by a little brook a mile up the trail, and then be ready for the "tug of war" on Monday.

In accordance with this plan, after eating our breakfast we each carried a light pack to our new camping ground, and there pitched our tent by a tiny brook that trickled down through the rocks. While Stanton cooked dinner, Pete brought forward a second pack. After we had eaten, Richards suggested to Pete that they take the fish net ahead and set it in the little lake which was still some two and a half miles farther on the trail. They had just returned when a terrific thunderstorm broke upon us, and every moment we expected the tent to be carried away by the gale that accompanied the downpour of rain. It was then that Richards remembered that he had left his blankets to dry upon the tepee poles at the last camp. The rain ceased about five o'clock, and Duncan volunteered to return with

Richards and help him recover his blankets, which they found far from dry.

Mosquitoes, it seemed to me, were never so numerous or vicious as after this thunderstorm. We had head nets that were a protection from them generally, but when we removed the nets to eat, the attacks of the insects were simply insufferable, so we had our supper in the tent. After our meal was finished and Pete had washed the dishes, I read aloud a chapter from the Bible--a Sunday custom that was maintained throughout the trip--and Stanton sang some hymns. Then we prevailed upon him to entertain us with other songs. He had an excellent tenor voice and a repertoire ranging from "The Holy City" to "My Brother Bob," and these and some of the old Scotch ballads, which he sang well, were favorites that he was often afterward called upon to render as we gathered around our evening camp fire, smoking our pipes and drinking in the tonic fragrance of the great solemn forest around us after a day of hard portaging. These impromptu concerts, storytelling, and reading aloud from two or three "vest pocket" classics that I carried, furnished our entertainment when we were not too tired to be amused.

The rain cleared the atmosphere, and Monday was cool and delightful, and, with the exception of two or three showers, a perfect day. Camp was moved and our entire outfit portaged to the first small lake. Our net, which Pete and Richards had set the day before, yielded us nothing, but with my rod I caught enough trout for a sumptuous supper.

The following morning (July fourth) Pete and I, who arose at half-past four, had just finished preparing breakfast of fried pork, flapjacks and coffee, and I had gone to the tent to call the others, when Pete came rushing after me in great excitement, exclaiming, "Caribou! Rifle quick!" He grabbed one of the 44's and rushed away and soon we heard bang-bang-bang seven times from up the lake shore. It was not long before Pete returned with a very humble bearing and crestfallen countenance, and without a word leaned the rifle against a tree and resumed his culinary operations.

"Well, Pete," said I, "how many caribou did you kill?"

"No caribou. Miss him," he replied.

"But I heard seven shots. How did you miss so many times?" I asked.

29

"Miss him," answered Pete. "I see caribou over there, close to water, run fast, try get lee side so he don't smell me. Water in way. Go very careful, make no noise, but he smell me. He hold his head up like this. He sniff, then he start. He go through trees very quick. See him, me, just little when he runs through trees. Shoot seven times. Hit him once, not much. He runs off. No good follow. Not hurt much, maybe goes very far."

"You had caribou fever, Pete," suggested Richards.

"Yes," said Easton, "caribou fever, sure thing."

"I don't believe you'd have hit him if he hadn't winded you," Stanton remarked. "The trouble with you, Pete, is you can't shoot."

"No caribou fever, me," rejoined Pete, with righteous indignation at such a suggestion. "Kill plenty moose, kill red deer; never have moose fever, never have deer fever." Then turning to me he asked, "You want caribou, Mr. Wallace?"

"Yes," I answered, "I wish we could get some fresh meat, but we can wait a few days. We have enough to eat, and I don't want to take time to hunt now."

"Plenty signs. I get caribou any day you want him. Tell me when you want him, I kill him," Pete answered me, ignoring the criticisms of the others as to his marksmanship and hunting prowess. All that day and all the next the men let no opportunity pass to guy Pete about his lost caribou, and on the whole he took the banter very good-naturedly, but once confided to me that "if those boys get up early, maybe they see caribou too and try how much they can do."

After breakfast Pete and I paddled to the other end of the little lake to pick up the trail while the others broke camp. In a little while he located it, a well-defined path, and we walked across it half a mile to another and considerably larger lake in which was a small, round, moundlike, spruce-covered island so characteristic of the Labrador lakes.

On our way back to the first lake Pete called my attention to a fresh caribou track in the hard earth. It was scarcely distinguishable, and I had to look very closely to make it out. Then he showed me other signs that I could make nothing of at all--a freshly turned pebble or broken twig. These, he said, were fresh deer signs. A caribou had passed toward the larger lake that very morning.

"If you want him, I get him," said Pete. I could see he felt rather deeply his failure of the morning and that he was anxious to redeem himself. I wanted to give him the opportunity to do so, especially as the young men, unused to deprivations, were beginning to crave fresh meat as a relief from the salt pork. At the same time, however, I felt that the fish we were pretty certain to get from this time on would do very well for the present, and I did not care to take time to hunt until we were a little deeper into the country. Therefore I told him, "No, we will wait a day or two."

Pete, as I soon discovered, had an insatiable passion for hunting, and could never let anything in the way of game pass him without qualms of regret. Sometimes, where a caribou trail ran off plain and clear in the moss, it was hard to keep from running after it. Nothing ever escaped his ear or eye. He had the trained senses and instincts of the Indian hunter. When I first saw him in New York he looked so youthful and evidently had so little confidence in himself, answering my question as to whether he could do this or that with an aggravating "I don't know," that I felt a keen sense of disappointment in him. But with every stage of our journey he had developed, and now was in his element. He was quite a different individual from the green Indian youth whom I had first seen walking timidly beside the railway conductor at the Grand Central Station in New York.

The portage between the lakes was an easy one and, as I have said, well defined, and we reached the farther shore of the second lake early in the afternoon. Here we found an old Indian camping ground covering several acres. It had evidently been at one time a general rendezvous of the Indians hunting in this section, as was indicated by the large number of wigwams that had been pitched here. That was a long while ago, however, for the old poles were so decayed that they fell into pieces when we attempted to pick them up.

There was no sign of a trail leading from the old camp ground, and I sent Pete and Richards to circle the bush and endeavor to locate one that I knew was somewhere about, while I fished and Stanton and Duncan prepared an early supper. A little later the two men returned, unsuccessful in their quest. They had seen two or three trails, any of which might be our trail. Of course but one of them could be the right one.

This report was both perplexing and annoying, for I did not wish to follow for several days a wrong route and then discover the error when much valuable time had been lost.

I therefore decided that we must be sure of our position before proceeding, and early the following morning dispatched Richards and Pete on a scouting expedition to a high hill some distance to the northeast that they might, from that view-point, note the general contour of the land and the location of any visible chain of lakes leading to the northwest through which the Indian trail might pass, and then endeavor to pick up the trail from one of these lakes, noting old camping grounds and other signs. As a precaution; in case they were detained overnight, each carried some tea and erbswurst, a rifle, a cup at his belt and a compass. When Pete took the rifle he held it up meaningly and said, "Fresh meat to-night. Caribou," and I could see that he was planning to make a hunt of it.

When they were gone, I took Easton with me and climbed another hill nearer camp so that I might get a panoramic view of the valley in which we were camped. From this vantage ground I could see, stretching off to the northward, a chain of three or four small lakes which, I concluded, though there was other water visible, undoubtedly marked our course. Far to the northwest was a group of rugged, barren, snowcapped mountains which were, perhaps, the "white hills," behind which the Indians had told us lay Seal Lake. At our feet, sparkling in the sunlight, spread the lake upon whose shores our tent, a little white dot amongst the green trees, was pitched. A bit of smoke curled up from our camp fire, where I knew Stanton and Duncan were baking "squaw bread."

We returned to camp to await the arrival and report of Richards and Pete, and occupied the afternoon in catching trout which, though more plentiful than in the first lake, were very small.

Toward evening, when a stiff breeze blew in from the lake and cleared the black flies and mosquitoes away. Easton took a canoe out, stripped, and sprang into the water, while I undressed on shore and was in the midst of a most refreshing bath when, suddenly, the wind died away and our tormentors came upon us in clouds. It was a scramble to get into our clothes again, but before I succeeded in hiding my nakedness from them, I was pretty severely wounded.

It was scarcely six o'clock when Richards and Pete walked into camp and proudly threw down some venison. Pete had kept his promise. On the lookout at every step for game, he had espied an old stag, and, together, he and Richards had stalked it, and it had received bullets from both their rifles. I shall not say to which hunter belonged the honor of killing the game. They were both very proud of it.

But best of all, they had found, to a certainty, the trail leading to one of the chain of little lakes which Easton and I had seen, and these lakes, they reported, took a course directly toward a larger lake, which they had glimpsed. I decided that this must be the lake of which the Indians at Northwest River had told us--Lake Nipishish (Little Water). This was very gratifying intelligence, as Nipishish was said to be nearly half way to Seal Lake, from where we had begun our portage on the Nascaupee.

What a supper we had that night of fresh venison, and new "squaw bread," hot from the pan!

In the morning we portaged our outfit two miles, and removed our camp to the second one of the series of lakes which Easton and I had seen from the hill, and the fourth lake after leaving the Nascaupee River. The morning was fearfully hot, and we floundered through marshes with heavy packs, bathed in perspiration, and fairly breathing flies and mosquitoes. Not a breath of air stirred, and the humidity and heat were awful. Stanton and Duncan remained to pitch the tent and bring up some of our stuff that had been left at the second lake, while Richards, Easton, Pete and I trudged three miles over the hills for the caribou meat which had been cached at the place where the animal was killed, Richards and Pete having brought with them only enough for two or three meals.

The country here was rough and broken, with many great boulders scattered over the hilltops. When we reached the cache we were ravenously hungry, and built a fire and had a very satisfying luncheon of broiled venison steak and tea. We bad barely finished our meal when heavy black clouds overcast the sky, and the wind and rain broke upon us in the fury of a hurricane. With the coming of the storm the temperature dropped fully forty degrees in half as many minutes, and in our dripping wet garments we were soon chilled and miserable. We hastened to cut the venison up and put it into packs, and with each a load of it, started homeward. On the way I stopped with Pete to climb a peak that I might have a view of the surrounding country and see the large lake to the northward which he and Richards had reported the evening before. The atmosphere was sufficiently clear by this time for me to see it, and I was satisfied that it was undoubtedly Lake Nipishish, as no other large lake had been mentioned by the Indians.

We hastened down the mountain and made our way through rain-soaked bushes and trees that showered us with their load of water at every step, and when at last we reached camp and I threw down my pack, I was too weary to change my wet garments for dry ones, and was glad to lie down, drenched as I was, to sleep until supper was ready.

None of our venison must be wasted. All that we could not use within the next day or two must be "jerked," that is, dried, to keep it from spoiling. To accomplish this we erected poles, like the poles of a wigwam, and suspended the meat from them, cut in thin strips, and in the center, between the poles, made a small, smoky fire to keep the greenbottle flies away, that they might not "blow" the venison, as well as to aid nature in the drying process.

All day on July seventh the rain poured down, a cold, northwest wind blew, and no progress was made in drying our meat. There was nothing to do but wait in the tent for the storm to clear.

When Pete went out to cook dinner I told him to make a little corn meal porridge and let it go at that, but what a surprise he had for us when, a little later, dripping wet and hands full of kettles, he pushed his way into the tent! A steaming venison potpie, broiled venison steaks, hot fried bread dough, stewed prunes for dessert and a kettle of hot tea! All experienced campers in the north woods are familiar with the fried bread dough. It is dough mixed as you would mix it for squaw bread, but not quite so stiff, pulled out to the size of your frying pan, very thin, and fried in swimming pork grease. In taste it resembles doughnuts. Hubbard used to call it "French toast." Our young men had never eaten it before, and Richards, taking one of the cakes, asked Pete:

"What do you call this?"

"I don't know," answered Pete.

"Well," said Richards, with a mouthful of it, "I call it darn good."

"That's what we call him then," retorted Pete, "darn good."

And so the cakes were christened "darn goods," and always afterward we referred to them by that name.

The forest fire which I have mentioned as having swept this country to the shores of Grand Lake some thirty-odd years ago, had been particularly destructive in this portion of the valley where we were now encamped. The stark dead spruce trees, naked skeletons of the old forest, stood all about, and that evening, when I stepped outside for a look at the sky and weather, I was impressed with the dreariness of the scene. The wind blew in gusts, driving the rain in sheets over the face of the hills and through the spectral trees, finally dashing it in bucketfuls against our tent.

The next forenoon, however, the sky cleared, and in the afternoon Richards and I went ahead in one of the canoes to hunt the trail. We followed the north shore of the lake to its end, then portaged twenty yards across a narrow neck into another lake, and keeping near the north shore of this lake also, continued until we came upon a creek of considerable size running out of it and taking a southeasterly course. Where the creek left the lake there was an old Indian fishing camp. It was out of the question that our trail should follow the valley of this creek, for it led directly away from our goal. We, therefore, returned and explored a portion of the north shore of the lake, which was very bare, boulder strewn, and devoid of vegetation for the most part--even moss.

Once we came upon a snow bank in a hollow, and cooled ourselves by eating some of the snow. Our observations made it quite certain that the trail left the northern side of the second lake through a boulder-strewn pass over the hills, though there were no visible signs of it, and we climbed one of the hills in the hope of seeing lakes beyond. There were none in sight. It was too late to continue our search that day and we reluctantly returned to camp. Our failure was rather discouraging because it meant a further loss of time, and I had hoped that our route, until we reached Nipishish at least, would lie straight and well defined before us.

Sunday was comfortably cool, with a good stiff breeze to drive away the flies. I dispatched Richards, with Pete and Easton to accompany him, to follow up our work of the evening before, and look into the pass through the hills, while I remained behind with Stanton and Duncan and kept the fire going under our venison.

I Had expected that Duncan, with his lifelong experience as a native trapper and hunter in the Labrador interior, would be of great assistance to us in locating the trail; but to my disappointment I discovered soon after our start that he was far from good even in following a trail when it was found, though he never got lost and could always find his way back, in a straight line, to any given point.

The boys returned toward evening and reported that beyond the hills, through the pass, lay a good-sized lake, and that some signs of a trail were found leading to it. This was what I had hoped for.

Our meat was now sufficiently dried to pack, and, anxious to be on the move again, I directed that on the morrow we should break camp and cross the hills to the lakes beyond.

Chapter 5: We Go Astray

At half-past four on Monday morning I called the men, and while Pete was preparing breakfast the rest of us broke camp and made ready for a prompt start. All were anxious to see behind the range of boulder-covered hills and to reach Lake Nipishish, which we felt could not now be far away. As soon as our meal was finished the larger canoe was loaded and started on ahead, while Richards, Duncan and I remained behind to load and follow in the other.

With the rising sun the day had become excessively warm, and there was not a breath of wind to cool the stifling atmosphere. The trail was ill-defined and rough, winding through bare glacial boulders that were thick-strewn on the ridges; and the difficulty of following it, together with the heat, made the work seem doubly hard, as we trudged with heavy packs to the shores of a little lake which nestled in a notch between the bills a mile and a half away. Once a fox ran before us and took refuge in its den under a large rock, but save the always present cloud of black flies, no other sign of life was visible on the treeless hills. Finally at midday, after three wearisome journeys back and forth, bathed in perspiration and dripping fly dope and pork grease, which we had rubbed on our faces pretty freely as a protection from the winged pests, we deposited our last load upon the shores of the lake, and thankfully stopped to rest and cook our dinner.

We were still eating when we heard the first rumblings of distant thunder and felt the first breath of wind from a bank of black clouds in the western sky, and had scarcely started forward again when the heavens opened upon us with a deluge.

The brunt of the storm soon passed, but a steady rain continued as we paddled through the lake and portaged across a short neck of land into a larger lake, down which we paddled to a small round island near its lower end. Here, drenched to the bone and thoroughly tired, we made camp, and in the shelter of the tent ate a savory stew composed of duck, grouse, venison and fat pork that Pete served in the most appetizing camp style.

I was astounded by the amount of squaw bread and "darn goods" that the young men of my party made away with, and began to fear not only for the flour supply, but also for the health of the men. One day when I saw one of my party eat three thick loaves of squaw bread in addition to a fair quantity of meat, I felt that it was time to limit the flour part of the ration. I expressed my fears to Pete, and advised that he bake less bread, and make the men eat more of the other food.

"Bread very good for Indian. Not good when white man eat so much. Good way fix him. Use not so much baking powder, me. Make him heavy," suggested Pete.

"No, Pete, use enough baking powder to make the bread good, and I'll speak to the men. Then if they don't eat less bread of their own accord, we'll have to limit them to a ration."

I decided to try this plan, and that evening in our camp on the island I told them that a ration of bread would soon have to be resorted to. They looked very solemn about it, for the bare possibility of a limited ration, something that they had never had to submit to, appeared like a hardship to them.

On Tuesday morning when we awoke the rain was still falling steadily. During the forenoon the storm abated somewhat and we broke camp and transferred our goods to the mainland, where the trail left the lake near a good-sized brook. Our portage led us over small bills and through marshes a mile and a half to another lake. While Pete remained at our new camp to prepare supper and Easton stayed with him, the rest of us brought forward the last load. Richards and I with a canoe and packs attempted to run down the brook, which emptied into the lake near our camp; but we soon found the stream too rocky, and were forced to cut our way through a dense growth of willows and carry the canoe and packs to camp on our backs.

The rain had ceased early in the afternoon, and the evening

was delightfully cool, so that the warmth of a big camp fire was most grateful and comforting. Our day's march had carried us into a well- wooded country, and the spectral dry sticks of the old burnt forest were behind us. The clouds hung low and threatening, and in the twilight beyond the glow of our leaping fire made the still waters of the lake, with its encircling wilderness of fir trees, seem very dark and somber. The genial warmth of the fire was so in contrast to the chilly darkness of the tent that we sat long around it and talked of our travels and prospects and the lake and the wilderness before us that no white man had ever before seen, while the brook near by tumbling over its rocky bed roared a constant complaint at our intrusion into this land of solitude.

The following morning was cool and fine, but showers developed during the day. Our venison, improperly dried, was molding, and much of it we found, upon unpacking, to be maggoty. After breakfast I instructed the others to cut out the wormy parts as far as possible and hang the good meat over the fire for further drying, while with Easton I explored a portion of the lake shore in search of the trail leading out. We returned for a late dinner, and then while Easton, Richards and I caught trout, I dispatched Pete and Stanton to continue the search beyond the point where Easton and I had left off. It was near evening when they came back with the information that they had found the trail, very difficult to follow, leading to a river, some two miles and a half beyond our camp. This was undoubtedly the Crooked River, which empties into Grand Lake close to the Nascaupee, and which the Indians had told us had its rise in Lake Nipishish.

The evening was very warm, and mosquitoes were so thick in the tent that we almost breathed them. Stanton, after much turning and fidgeting, finally took his blanket out of doors, where he said it was cooler and he could sleep with his head covered to protect him; but in an hour he was back, and with his blanket wet with dew took his usual place beside me.

Below the point where the trail enters the Crooked River it is said by the Indians to be exceedingly rough and entirely impassable. We portaged into it the next morning, paddled a short distance up the stream, which is here some two hundred yards in width and rather shallow, then poled through a short rapid and tracked through two others, wading almost to our waists in some places. We now came to a widening of the river where it spread out into a small lake. Near the upper end of this expansion was an island upon which we found a long- disused log cache of the Indians. A little distance above the island what appeared to be two rivers flowed into the expansion. Richards, Duncan and I explored up the right-hand branch until we struck a rapid. Upon our return to the point where the two streams came together we found that the other canoe, against my positive instructions not to proceed at uncertain points until I had decided upon the proper route to take, had gone up the branch on the left, tracked through a rapid and disappeared.

There were no signs of Indians on either of these branches so far as we could discover, and I was well satisfied that somewhere on the north bank of the expansion, probably not far from the island and old cache which we had passed, was the trail. But evening was coming on and rain was threatening, so there was nothing to do but follow the other canoe, which had gone blindly ahead, until we should overtake it, as it contained all the cooking utensils and our tent. This failure of the men to obey instructions took us a considerable distance out of our way and cost us several days' time, as we discovered later.

We tracked through some rapids and finally overhauled the others at a place where the river branched again. It was after seven o'clock, a drizzling rain was falling, and here we pitched camp on the east side of the river just opposite the junction of the two branches.

On the west fork and directly across from our camp was a rough rapid, and while supper was cooking I paddled over with Richards to try for fish. We made our casts, and I quickly landed a twenty-inch ouananiche and Richards hooked a big trout that, after much play, was brought ashore. It measured twenty-two and a half inches from tip to tip and eleven and a half inches around the shoulders. I had landed a couple more large trout, when Richards enthusiastically announced that he had a big fellow hooked. He played the fish for half an hour before he brought it to the edge of the rock, so completely exhausted that it could scarcely move a fin. We had no landing net and he attempted to lift it out by the line, when snap went the hook and the fish was free! I made a dash, caught it in my hands and triumphantly brought it ashore. It proved to be an ouananiche that measured twenty-seven and one-half inches in length by eleven and one-quarter inches in girth.

In our excitement we had forgotten all about supper and did not even know that it was raining; but we now saw Pete on the further shore gesticulating wildly and pointing at his open mouth, in pantomime suggestion that the meal was waiting.

"Well, that is fishing!" remarked Richards. "I never landed a fish as big as that before."

"Yes," I answered; "we're getting near the headwaters of the river now, where the big fish are always found."

"I never expected any such sport as that. It's worth the hard work just for this hour's fishing."

"You'll get plenty more of it before we're through the country. There are some big fellows under that rapid. The Indians told us we should find salmon in this section too, but we're ahead of the salmon, I think. They're hardly due for a month yet."

"Let's show the fellows the trout, first. They're big enough to make 'em open their eyes. Then we'll spring the ouananiche on 'cm and they'll faint. It'll, be enough to make Easton want to come and try a cast too."

So when we pushed through the dripping bushes to the tent we presented only the few big trout, which did indeed create a sensation. Then Richards brought forward his ouananiche, and it produced the desired effect. After supper Pete and Easton must try their hand at the fish, and they succeeded in catching five trout averaging, we estimated, from two to three pounds each. Richards, however, still held the record as to big fish, both trout and ouananiche, and the others vowed they would take it from him if they had to fish nights to do it.

En route up the river, in the afternoon, Pete had shot a muskrat, and I asked him that night what he was going to do with it.

"I don't know," he answered. "Muskrat no good now."

"Well, never kill any animal while you are with me that you cannot use, except beasts of prey."

This was one of the rules that I had laid down at the beginning: that no member of the party should kill for the sake of killing any living thing. I could not be angry with Pete, however, for he was always so good-natured. No matter how

41

sharply I might reprove him, in five minutes he would be doing something for my comfort, or singing some Indian song as he went lightheartedly about his work. I understood how hard it was for him to down the Indian instinct to kill, and that the muskrat bad been shot thoughtlessly without considering for a moment whether it were needed or not. The flesh of the muskrat at this season of the year is very strong in flavor and unpalatable, and besides, with the grouse that were occasionally killed, the fish that we were catching, and the dried venison still on hand, we could not well use it. No fur is, of course, in season at this time of year, and so there was no excuse for killing muskrats for the pelts.

In the vicinity of this camp we saw some of the largest spruce timber that we came upon in the whole journey across Labrador. Some of these trees were fully twenty-two inches in diameter at the butt and perhaps fifty to sixty feet in height. These large trees were very scattered, however, and too few to be of commercial value. For the most part the trees that we met with were six to eight, and, occasionally, ten inches through, scrubby and knotted. In Labrador trees worth the cutting are always located near streams in sheltered valleys.

That evening before we retired the drizzle turned to a downpour, and we were glad to leave our unprotected camp fire for the unwarmed shelter of our tent. While I lay within and listened to the storm, I wrote in my diary: "As I lie here, the rain pours upon the tent over my head and drip--drip--drips through small holes in the silk; the wind sweeps through the spruce trees outside and a breath of the fragrance of the great damp forest comes to me. I hear the roar of the rapid across the river as the waters pour down over the rocks in their course to the sea. I wonder if some of those very waters do not wash the shores of New York. How far away the city seems, and how glad I shall be to return home when my work here is finished!

"This is a feeling that comes to one often in the wilderness. Perhaps it is a touch of homesickness--a hunger for the sympathy and companionship of our friends."

The days that followed were days of weary waiting and inactivity. A cold northeast storm was blowing and the rain fell heavily and incessantly day and night. Trail hunting was impracticable while the storm lasted, but the halt offered an opportunity that was taken advantage of to repair our outfit; also there was much needed mending to be done, as some of our clothing was badly torn.

Everything we had in the way of wearing apparel was wet, and we set up our tent stove for the first time, that we might dry our things under cover. This stove proved a great comfort to us, and all agreed that it was an inspiration that led me to bring it. It was not an inspiration, however, but my experience on the trip with Hubbard that taught the necessity of a stove for just such occasions as this, and for the colder weather later.

Some of us went to the rapid to fish, but it was too cold for either fly or bait, and we soon gave it up. I slipped off a rock in the lower swirl of the rapid, and went into the river over my head and ears. Pete, who was with me, gave audible expression to his amusement at my discomfiture as I crawled out of the water like a half drowned rat; but I could see no occasion for his hilarity and I told him so.

This experience dampened my enthusiasm as a fisherman for that day. The net was set, however, which later yielded us some trout. A fish planked on a dry spruce log hewn flat on one side, made a delicious dinner, and a savory kettle of fish chowder made of trout and dried onions gave us an equally good supper.

On July fifteenth sleet was mingled with the rain in the early morning, and it was so cold that Duncan used his mittens when doing outdoor work. Easton was not feeling well, and I looked upon our delay as not altogether lost time, as it gave him an opportunity to get into shape again.

A pocket copy of "Hiawatha," from which Stanton read aloud, furnished us with entertainment. Pete was very much interested in the reading, and I found he was quite familiar with the legends of his Indian hero, and he told us some stories of Hiawatha that I had never heard. "Hiawatha," said Pete, "he the same as Christ. He do anything he want to." Pete produced his harmonica and proved himself a very good performer.

July sixteenth was Sunday, and I decided that rain or shine we must break camp on Monday and move forwards for the inactivity was becoming unendurable.

A little fishing was done, and Pete landed a twenty-two and three- quarter inch trout, thus wresting the big-trout record from Richards. Pete was proud and boasted a great deal of this feat, which he claimed proved his greater skill as a fisherman, but which the others attributed to luck.

We were enabled to do some scouting in the afternoon, which resulted in the discovery that our camp was on an island. Nowhere could we find any Indian signs, and we were therefore quite evidently off the trail.

Chapter 6: Lake Nipishish is Reached

As already stated, the Indians at Northwest River Post had informed us that the Crooked River had its rise in Lake Nipishish, and I therefore decided to follow the stream from the point where we were now encamped to the lake, or until we should come upon the trail again, as I felt sure we should do farther up, rather than retrace our steps to the abandoned cache on the island in the expansion below, and probably consume considerable time in locating the old portage route from that point.

Accordingly, on Monday morning we began our work against the almost continuous rapids, which we discovered as we proceeded were characteristic of the river. A heavy growth of willows lined the banks, forcing us into the icy water, where the swift current made it very difficult to keep our footing upon the slippery boulders of the river bed. Tracking lines were attached to the bows of the canoes and we floundered forward.

The morning was cloudy and cool and resembled a day in late October, but before noon the sun graciously made his appearance and gave us new spirit for our work. When we stopped for dinner I sent Pete and Easton to look ahead, and Pete brought back the intelligence that a half-mile portage would cut off a considerable bend in the river and take us into still water. It was necessary to clear a portion of the way with the ax. This done, the portage was made, and then we found to our disappointment that the still water was less than a quarter mile in length, when rapids occurred again.

As I deemed it wise to get an idea of the lay of the land before proceeding farther, I took Pete with me and went ahead to scout

45

the route. Less than a mile away we found two small lakes, and climbing a ridge two miles farther on, we had a view of the river, which, so far as we could see, continued to be very rough, taking a turn to the westward above where our canoes were stationed, and then swinging again to the northeast in the direction of Nipishish, which was plainly visible. The Indians, instead of taking the longer route that we were following, undoubtedly crossed from the old cache to a point in the river some distance above where it took its westward swing, and thus, in one comparatively easy portage, saved themselves several miles of rough traveling. It was too late for us now, however, to take advantage of this.

Pete and I hurried back to the others. The afternoon was well advanced, but sufficient daylight remained to permit us to proceed a little way up the river, and portage to the shores of one of the lakes, where camp was made just at dusk.

Field mice in this section were exceedingly troublesome. They would run over us at night, sample our food, and gnawed a hole as large as a man's hand in the side of the tent. Porcupines, too, were something of a nuisance. One night one of them ate a piece out of my tumpline, which was partially under my head, while I slept.

The next morning we passed through the lakes to the river above, and for three days, in spite of an almost continuous rain and wind storm, worked our way up stream, "tracking" the canoes through a succession of rapids or portaging around them, with scarcely any opportunity to paddle.

On the afternoon of the third day, with the wind dashing the rain in sheets into our faces, we halted on a rough piece of ground just above the river bank and pitched our tent.

When camp was made Pete took me to a rise of ground a little distance away, and pointing to the northward exclaimed: "Look, Lake Nipishish! I know we reach him today."

And sure enough, there lay Lake Nipishish close at hand! I was more thankful than I can say to see the water stretching far away to the northward, for I felt that now the hardest and roughest part of our journey to the height of land was completed.

"That's great, Pete," said I. "We'll have more water after this and fewer and easier portages, and we can travel faster."

46

"Maybe better, I don't know," remarked Pete, rather skeptically. "Always hard find trail out big lakes. May leave plenty places. Take more time hunt trail maybe now. Indian maps no good. Maybe easier when we find him."

Pete was right, and I did not know the difficulties still to be met with before we should reach Michikamau.

Duncan was of comparatively little help to us now, and as I knew that he was more than anxious to return to Groswater Bay, I decided to dispense with his further services and send him back with letters to be mailed home. When I returned to the tent I said to him:

"Duncan, I suppose you would like to go home now, and I will let you turn back from here and take some letters out. Does that suit you?"

"Yes, sir, that suits me fine," replied be promptly, and in a tone that left no doubt of the fact that he was glad to go.

"Well, this is Thursday. I'll write my letters tomorrow, and you may go on Saturday."

"All right, sir."

The letters were all written and ready for Duncan on Friday night, and he packed sufficient provisions into a waterproof bag I gave him to carry him out, and prepared for an early start in the morning. But the rain that had been falling for several days still poured down on Saturday, and he decided to postpone his departure another day in the hope of better weather on Sunday. He needed the time anyway to mend his sealskin boots before starting back, for he had pretty nearly worn them out on the sharp rocks on the portages. The rest of us were well provided with oil-tanned moccasins (sometimes called larigans or shoe-packs), which I have found are the best footwear for a journey like ours. Pete's khaki trousers were badly torn; and Richards and Easton, who wore Mackinaw trousers, were in rags. This cloth had not withstood the hard usage of Labrador travel a week, and both men, when they bad a spare hour, occupied it in sewing on canvas patches, until now there was almost as much canvas patch as Mackinaw cloth in these garments. Richards, however, carried an extra pair of moleskin trousers, and I wore moleskin. This latter material is the best obtainable, so far as my experience goes, for rough traveling in the bush, and my trousers stood the trip with but one small patch until winter came.

Sunday morning was still stormy, but before noon the rain ceased, and Duncan announced his intention of starting homeward at once. We raised our flags and exchanged our farewells and Godspeeds with him. Then he left us, and as be disappeared down the trail a strange sense of loneliness came upon us, for it seemed to us that his going broke the last link that connected us with the outside world. Duncan was always so cheerful, with his quaint humor, and so ready to do his work to the very best of his ability, that we missed him very much, and often spoke of him in the days that followed.

We had made the best of our enforced idleness in this camp to repack and condense and dry our outfit as much as possible. The venison, at the first imperfectly cured, had been so continuously soaked that the most of what remained of it was badly spoiled and we could not use it, and with regret we threw it away. The erbswurst was also damp, and this we put into small canvas bags, which were then placed near the stove to dry.

A rising barometer augured good weather for Monday morning. A light wind scattered the clouds that had for so many days entombed the world in storm and gloom, and the sun broke out gloriously, setting the moisture-laden trees aglinting as though hung with a million pearls and warming the damp fir trees until the air was laden with the forest perfume. It was as though a pall had been lifted from the world. How our hearts swelled with the new enthusiasm of the returned sunshine! It was always so. It seemed as if the long-continued storms bound up our hearts and crushed the buoyancy from them; but the returning sunshine melted the bonds at once and gave us new ambition. A robin sang gayly from a near-by tree--a messenger from the kindlier Southland come to cheer us--and the "whisky jacks," who had not shown themselves for several days, appeared again with their shrill cries, venturing impudently into the very door of our tent to claim scraps of refuse.

I was for moving forward that very afternoon, but some of our things were still wet, and I deemed it better judgment to let them have the day in which to dry and to delay our start until Monday morning.

After supper, in accordance with the Sunday custom established by Hubbard when I was with him, I read aloud a selection from the Testament--the last chapter of Revelation--and then went out of the tent to take the usual nine o'clock weather observation. Between the horizon and a fringe of black clouds that hung low in the north the reflected sun set the heavens afire, and through the dark fir trees the lake stretched red as a lake of blood. I called the others to see it and Easton joined me. We climbed a low hill close at hand to view the scene, and while we looked the red faded into orange, and the lake was transformed into a mirror, which reflected the surrounding trees like an inverted forest. In the direction from which we had come we could see the high blue hills beyond the Nascaupee, very dim in the far distance. Below us the Crooked River lost itself as it wound its tortuous way through the wooded valley that we had traversed. Somewhere down there Duncan was bivouacked, and we wondered if his fire was burning at one of our old camping places.

Darkness soon came and we returned to the tent to find the others rolled in their blankets, and we joined them at once that we might have a good night's rest preparatory to an early morning advance.

Before seven o'clock on Monday morning (July twenty-fourth) we had made our portage to the water that we had supposed to be an arm of Lake Nipishish, but which proved instead to be an expansion of the river into which the lake poured its waters through a short rapid. This rapid necessitated another short portage before we were actually afloat upon the bosom of Nipishish itself. There was not a cloud to mar the azure of the sky, hardly a breath of wind to make a ripple on the surface of the lake, and the morning was just cool enough to be delightful.

It was the kind of day and kind of wilderness that makes one want to go on and on. I felt again the thrill in my blood of that magic something that had held possession of Hubbard and me and lured us into the heart of this unknown land two years before, and as I looked hungrily away toward the hills to the northward, I found myself repeating again one of those selections from Kipling that I had learned from him:

"Something hidden. Go and find it. Go and look behind the Ranges-- Something lost behind the Ranges. Lost and waiting for you. Go!"

Chapter 7: Scouting for the Trail

Lake Nipishish is approximately twenty miles in length, and at its broadest part ten or twelve miles in width. It extends in an almost due easterly direction from the place where we launched our canoes near its outlet. The shores are rocky and rise gradually into low, well-wooded hills, by which the lake is surrounded. Five miles from the outlet a rocky point juts out into the water, and above the point an arm of the lake reaches into the hills to the northward to a distance of six miles, almost at right angles to the main lake. In the arm there are several small, rocky islands which sustain a scrubby growth of black spruce and fir balsam.

Hitherto the Indian maps had been of little assistance to us. No estimate of distance could be made from them, and the lakes through which we had passed (not all of them shown on the map) were represented by small circles with nothing to indicate at what point on their shores the trail was to be found. Lake Nipishish, however, was drawn on a larger scale and with more detail, and we readily located the trail leading out of the arm which I have mentioned.

After a day's work through several small lakes or ponds, with short intervening portages, and a trail on the whole well defined and easily followed, we came one afternoon to a good-sized lake of irregular shape which Pete promptly named Washkagama (Crooked Lake).

A stream flowed into Washkagama near the place where we went ashore, and it seemed to me probable that our route might be along this stream, which it was likely drained lakes farther up; but a search in the vicinity failed to uncover any signs of the trail, and the irregular shape of the lake suggested several other likely places for it. We were, therefore, forced to go into camp, disappointing as it was, until we should know our position to a certainty.

The next day was showery, but we began in the morning a determined hunt for the trail. Stanton remained in camp to make needed repairs to the outfit; Easton went with Pete to the northward, while Richards and I in one of the canoes paddled to the eastern side of the lake arm, upon which we were encamped, to climb a barren hill from which we hoped to get a good view of the country, and upon reaching the summit we were not disappointed. A wide panorama was spread before us. To the north lay a great rolling country covered with a limitless forest of firs, with here and there a bit of sparkling water. A mile from our camp a creek, now and again losing itself in the green woods, rushed down to join Washkagama, anxious to gain the repose of the lake. To the northeast the rugged white hills that we were hoping to reach soon, loomed up grand and majestic, with patches of snow, like white sheets, spread over their sides and tops. From Nipishish to Washkagama we had passed through a burned and rocky country where no new growth save scant underbrush and a few scattering spruce, balsam and tamarack trees had taken the place of the old destroyed forest. The dead, naked tree trunks which, gaunt and weather-beaten, still stood upright or lay in promiscuous confusion on the ground, gave this part of the country from our hilltop view an appearance of solitary desolation that we had not noticed when we were traveling through it. But this unregenerated district ended at Washkagama; and below it Nipishish, with its green-topped hills, seemed almost homelike.

The creek that I have mentioned as flowing into the lake a mile from our camp seemed to me worthy to be explored for the trail, and I determined to go there at once upon our return to camp, while Richards desired to climb a rock-topped hill which held its head above the timber line three or four miles to the northwest, that he might make topographical and geological observations there.

We returned to camp, and Richards, with a package of erbswurst in his pocket to cook for dinner and my rifle on his shoulder, started immediately into the bush, and was but just gone when Pete and Easton appeared with the report that two miles above us lay a large lake, and that they had found the trail leading from it to the creek I had seen from the hill. The lake lay among the hills to the northward, and the bits of water I had seen were portions of it. I was anxious to break camp and start forward, but this could not be done until Richards' return. Easton, Pete and I paddled up to the creek's mouth, therefore, and spent the day fishing, and landed eighty-seven trout, ranging from a quarter pound to four pounds in weight. The largest ones Stanton split and hung over the fire to dry for future use, while the others were applied to immediate need.

When Richards came into camp in the evening he brought with him an excellent map of the country that he had seen from the hill and reported having counted ten lakes, including the large one that Easton and Pete had visited. He also had found the trail and followed it back.

The next morning some tracking and wading up the creek was necessary before we found ourselves upon the trail with packs on our backs, and before twelve o'clock we arrived with all our outfit at the lake, which we shall call Minisinaqua. It was an exceedingly beautiful sheet of water, the main body, perhaps, ten or twelve miles in length, but narrow, and with many arms and indentations and containing numerous round green islands. The shores and surrounding country were well wooded with spruce, fir, balsam, larch, and an occasional small white birch.

I took my place in the larger canoe with Pete and Easton and left Stanton to follow with Richards. Pete's eyes, as always, were scanning with keen scrutiny every inch of shore. Suddenly he straightened up, peered closely at an island, and in a stage whisper exclaimed "Caribou! Caribou! Don't make noise! Paddle, quick!"

We saw them then--two old stags and a fawn--on an island, but they had seen us, too, or winded us more likely, and, rushing across the island, took to the water on the opposite side, making for the mainland. We bent to our paddles with all our might, hoping to get within shooting distance of them, but they had too much lead. We all tried some shots when we saw we could not get closer, but the deer were five hundred yards away, and from extra exertion with our paddles, we were unable to hold steady, and missed.

Our canoes were turned into an arm of the lake leading to the northward. Amongst some islands we came upon a flock of five geese-- two old ones and three young ones. The old ones had just passed through the molting season, and their new wing feathers were not long enough to bear them, and the young ones, though nearly full grown, had not yet learned to fly. Pete brought the mother goose and two of her children down with the shotgun, but father gander and the other youngster escaped, flapping away on the surface of the lake at a remarkable speed, and they were allowed to go with their lives without a chase.

We stumbled upon the trail leading from Lake Minisinaqua, almost immediately upon landing. Its course was in a northerly direction through the valley of a small river that emptied into the lake. This valley was inclosed by low hills, and the country, like that between Washkagama and Lake Minisinaqua, was well covered with the same varieties of small trees that were found there. For a mile and three- quarters, the stream along which the trail ran was too swift for canoeing, but it then expanded into miniature lakes or ponds which were connected by short rapids. Each of us portaged a load to the first pond, where the canoes were to be launched, and I directed Pete and Stanton to remain here, pluck the geese, and prepare two of them for an evening dinner, while Richards, Easton and I brought forward a second load and pitched camp.

This was Easton's twenty-second birthday and it occurred to me that it would be a pleasant variation to give a birthday dinner in his honor and to have a sort of feast to relieve the monotony of our daily life, and give the men something to think about and revive their spirits; for "bucking the trail" day after day with no change but the gradual change of scenery does grow monotonous to most men, and the ardor of the best of them, especially men unaccustomed to roughing it, will become damped in time unless some variety, no matter how slight, can be brought into their lives. A good dinner always has this effect, for after men are immersed in a wilderness for several weeks, good things to eat take the first place in their thoughts and, to judge from their conversation, the attainment of these is their chief aim in life.

My instructions to Pete included the baking of an extra ration of bread to be served hot with the roast geese, and I asked Stanton to try his hand at concocting some kind of a pudding out of the few prunes that still remained, to be served with sugar as sauce, and accompanied by black coffee. Our coffee supply was small and it was used only on Sundays now, or at times when we desired an especial treat.

We were pretty tired when we returned with our second packs and dropped them on a low, bare knoll some fifty yards above the fire where Pete and Stanton were carrying on their culinary operations, but a whiff of roasting goose came to us like a tonic, and it did not take us long to get camp pitched.

"Um-m-m," said Easton, stopping in his work of driving tent pegs to sniff the air now bearing to us appetizing odors of goose and coffee, "that smells like home."

"You bet it does," assented Richards. "I haven't been filled up for a week, but I'm going to be to-night."

At length dinner was ready, and we fell to with such good purpose that the two birds, a generous portion of hot bread, innumerable cups of black coffee, and finally, a most excellent pudding that Stanton had made out of bread dough and prunes and boiled in a canvas specimen bag disappeared.

How we enjoyed it! "No hotel ever served such a banquet," one of the boys remarked as we filled our pipes and lighted them with brands from the fire. Then with that blissful feeling that nothing but a good dinner can give, we lay at full length on the deep white moss, peace- fully puffing smoke at the stars as they blinked sleepily one by one out of the blue of the great arch above us until the whole firmament was glittering with a mass of sparkling heaven gems. The soft perfume of the forest pervaded the atmosphere; the aurora borealis appeared in the northern sky, and its waves of changing light swept the heavens; the vast silence of the wilderness possessed the world and, wrapped in his own thoughts, no man spoke to break the spell. Finally Pete began a snatch of Indian song:

"Puhgedewawa enenewug Nuhbuggesug kamiwauw."

Then he drew from his pocket a harmonica, and for half an hour played soft music that harmonized well with the night and the surroundings; when he ceased, all but Richards and I went to their blankets. We two remained by the dying embers of our fire for another hour to enjoy the perfect night, and then, before we turned to our beds, made an observation for compass variation, which calculations the following morning showed to be thirty-seven degrees west of the true north.

Paddling through the ponds, polling and tracking through the rapids or portaging around them up the little river on which we were encamped the night before, brought us to Otter Lake, which was considerably larger than Lake Minisinaqua, but not so large as Nipishish. The main body was not over a mile and a half in width, but it had a number of bays and closely connected tributary lakes. Its eastern end, which we did not explore, penetrated low spruce and balsam-covered hills. To the north and northeast were rugged, rock-tipped hills, rising to an elevation of some seven hundred feet above the lake. The country at their base was covered with a green forest of small fir, spruce and birch, and near the water, in marshy places, as is the case nearly everywhere in Labrador, tamarack, but the hills themselves had been fire swept, and were gray with weather-worn, dead trees. On the summits, and for two hundred feet below, bare basaltic rock indicated that at this elevation they had never sustained any growth, save a few straggling bushes. On some of these hills there still remained patches of snow of the previous winter.

We paddled eastward along the northern shore of the lake. Once we saw a caribou swimming far ahead of us, but he discovered our approach and took to the timber before we were within shooting distance of him. A flock of sawbill ducks avoided us. No sign of Indians was seen, and four miles up the lake we stopped upon a narrow, sandy point that jutted out into the water for a distance of a quarter mile, to pitch camp and scout for the trail. All along the point and leading back into the bush, were fresh caribou tracks, where the animals came out to get the benefit of the lake breezes and avoid the flies, which torment them terribly. Natives in the North have told me of caribou having been worried to death by the insects, and it is not improbable. The "bulldogs" or "stouts," as they are sometimes called, which are as big as bumblebees, are very vicious, and follow the poor caribou in swarms. The next morning a caribou wandered down to within a hundred and fifty yards of camp, and Pete and Stanton both fired at it, but missed, and it got away unscathed.

After breakfast, with Pete and Easton, I climbed one of the higher hills for a view of the surrounding country. Near the foot of the hill, and in the depth of the spruce woods, we passed a lone Indian grave, which we judged from its size to be that of a child. It was inclosed by a rough fence, which had withstood the pressure of the heavy snows of many winters and a broken cross lay on it. From the summit of the hill we could see a string of lakes extending in a general northwesterly direction until they were lost in other hills above, and also numerous lakes to the south, southwest, east and northeast. We could count from one point nearly fifty of these lakes, large and small. To the north and northwest the country was rougher and more diversified, and the hills much higher than any we had as yet passed through.

Down by our camp it had been excessively warm, but here on the hilltop a cold wind was blowing that made us shiver. We found a few scattered dry sticks, and built a fire under the lee of a high boulder, where we cooked for luncheon some pea-meal porridge with water that Pete, with foresight, had brought with him from a brook that we passed half way down the hillside. We then continued our scouting tour several miles inland, climbing two other high hills, from one of which an excellent view was had of the string of lakes penetrating the northwestern hills. Everywhere so far as our vision extended the valleys were comparatively well wooded, but the treeless, rock-bound hills rose grimly above the timber line.

When we returned to camp we were still unsettled as to where the trail left the lake, but there was one promising bay that had not been explored, and Richards and Easton volunteered to take a canoe and search this bay. They were supplied with tarpaulin, blankets, an ax and one day's rations, and started immediately.

I felt some anxiety as to our slow progress. August was almost upon us and we had not yet reached Seal Lake. Here, as at other places, we had experienced much delay in finding the trail, and we did not know what difficulties in that direction lay before us. I had planned to reach the George River by early

September, and the question as to whether we could do it or not was giving me much concern.

Pete and Stanton had been in bed and asleep for an hour, but I was still awake, turning over in my mind the situation, and planning tomorrow's campaign, when at ten o'clock I heard the soft dip of paddles, and a few moments later Richards and Easton appeared out of the night mist that hung over the lake, with the good news that they had found the trail leading northward from the bay.

Chapter 8: Seal Lake at Last

A thick, impenetrable mist, such as is seldom seen in the interior of Labrador, hung over the water and the land when we struck camp and began our advance. For two days we traveled through numerous small lakes, making several short portages, before we came to a lake which we found to be the headwaters of a river flowing to the northwest. This lake was two miles long, and we camped at its lower end, where the river left it. Portage Lake we shall call it, and the river that flowed out of it Babewendigash.

The portage into the lake crossed a sand desert, upon which not a drop of water was seen, and instead of the usual rocks there were uncovered sand and gravel knolls and valleys, where grew only occasional bunches of very stunted brush; the surface of the sand was otherwise quite bare and sustained not even the customary moss and lichens. The heat of the sun reflected from the sand was powerful. The day was one of the most trying ones of the trip, and the men, with faces and hands swollen and bleeding from the attacks of not only the small black flies, which were particularly bad, but also the swarms of "bulldogs," complained bitterly of the hardships. When we halted to eat our luncheon one of the men remarked, "Duncan said once that if there are no flies there, hell can't be as bad as this, and he's pretty near right."

The river left the lake in a rapid, and while Pete was making his fire, Richards, Easton and I went down to catch our supper, and in half an hour had secured forty-five good-sized trout-- sufficient for supper that night and breakfast and dinner the next day.

Since leaving Otter Lake, caribou signs had been plentiful, fresh trails running in every direction. Pete was anxious to halt a day to hunt, but I decreed otherwise, to his great disappointment.

The scenery at this point was particularly fine, with a rugged, wild beauty that could hardly be surpassed. Below us the great, bald snow hills loomed very close at hand, with patches of snow glinting against the black rocks of the hills, as the last rays of the setting sun kissed them good-night. Nearer by was the more hospitable wooded valley and the shining river, and above us the lake, placid and beautiful, and beyond it the line of low sand hills of the miniature desert we had crossed. One of the snow hills to the northwest had two knobs resembling a camel's back, and was a prominent landmark. We christened it "The Camel's Hump."

Heretofore the streams had been taking a generally southerly direction, but this river flowed to the northwest, which was most encouraging, for running in that direction it could have but one outlet-the Nascaupee River.

A portage in the morning, then a short run on the river, then another portage, around a shallow rapid, and we were afloat again on one of the prettiest little rivers I have ever seen. The current was strong enough to hurry us along. Down we shot past the great white hills, which towered in majestic grandeur high above our heads, in some places rising almost perpendicularly from the water, with immense heaps of debris which the frost had detached from their sides lying at their base. The river was about fifty yards wide, and in its windings in and out among the hills almost doubled upon itself sometimes. The scenery was fascinating. One or two small lake expansions were passed, but generally there was a steady current and a good depth of water. "This is glorious!" someone exclaimed, as we shot onward, and we all appreciated the relief from the constant portaging that had been the feature of our journey since leaving the Nascaupee River.

The first camp on this river was pitched upon the site of an old Indian camp, above a shallow rapid. The many wigwam poles, in varying states of decay, together with paddles, old snowshoes, broken sled runners, and other articles of Indian traveling paraphernalia, indicated that it had been a regular stopping place of the Indians, both in winter and in summer, in the days when they had made their pilgrimages to Northwest River Post. Near this point we found some beaver cuttings, the first that we had seen since leaving the Crooked River.

Babewendigash soon carried us into a large lake expansion, and six hours were consumed paddling about the lake before the outlet was discovered. At first we thought it possible we were in Seal Lake, but I soon decided that it was not large enough, and its shape did not agree with the description of Seal Lake that Donald Blake and Duncan McLean had given me.

During the morning I dropped a troll and landed the first namaycush of the trip--a seven-pound fish. The Labrador lakes generally have a great depth of water, and it is in the deeper water that the very large namaycush, which grow to an immense size, are to be caught. Our outfit did not contain the heavy sinkers and larger trolling spoons necessary in trolling for these, and we therefore had to content ourselves with the smaller fish caught in the shallower parts of the lakes. We had two more portages before we shot the first rapid of the trip, and then camped on the shores of a small expansion just above a wide, shallow rapid where the river swung around a ridge of sand hills. This ridge was about two hundred feet in elevation, and followed the river for some distance below. In the morning we climbed it, and walked along its top for a mile or so, to view the rapid, and suddenly, to the westward, beheld Seal Lake. It was a great moment, and we took off our hats and cheered. The first part of our fight up the long trail was almost ended.

The upper part of the rapid was too shallow to risk a full load in the canoes, so we carried a part of our outfit over the ridge to a point where the river narrowed and deepened, then ran the rapid and picked up our stuff below. Not far from here we passed a hill whose head took the form of a sphinx and we noted it as a remarkable landmark. Stopping but once to climb a mountain for specimens, at twelve o'clock we landed on a sandy beach where Babewendigash River emptied its waters into Seal Lake. We could hardly believe our good fortune, and while Pete cooked dinner I climbed a hill to satisfy myself that it was really Seal Lake. There was no doubt of it. It had been very minutely described and sketched for me by Donald and Duncan. We had halted at what they called on their maps "The

Narrows," where the lake narrowed down to a mere strait, and that portion of it below the canoes was hidden from my view. It stretched out far to the northwest, with some distance up a long arm reaching to the west. A point which I recognized from Duncan's description as the place where the winter tilt used by him and Donald was situated extended for some distance out into the water. The entire length of Seal Lake is about forty miles, but only about thirty miles of it could be seen from the elevation upon which I stood. Its shores are generally well wooded with a growth of young spruce. High hills surround it.

We visited the tilt as we passed the point and, in accordance with an arrangement made with Duncan, added to our stores about twenty-five pounds of flour that he had left there during the previous winter. Five miles above the point where Babewendigash River empties into Seal Lake we entered the Nascaupee, up which we paddled two miles to the first short rapid. This we tracked, and then made camp on an island where the river lay placid and the wind blew cool and refreshing.

Long we sat about our camp fire watching the glories of the northern sunset, and the new moon drop behind the spruce-clad hills, and the aurora in all its magnificence light our silent world with its wondrous fire. Finally the others left me to go to their blankets.

When I was alone I pushed in the ends of the burning logs and sat down to watch the blaze as it took on new life. Gradually, as I gazed into its depths, fantasy brought before my eyes the picture of another camp fire. Hubbard was sitting by it. It was one of those nights in the hated Susan Valley. We had been toiling up the trail for days, and were ill and almost disheartened; but our camp fire and the relaxation from the day's work were giving us the renewed hope and cheer that they always brought, and rekindled the fire of our half-lost enthusiasm. "Seal Lake can't be far off now," Hubbard was saying. "We're sure to reach it in a day or two. Then it'll be easy work to Michikamau, and we 'll soon be with the Indians after that, and forget all about this hard work. We'll be glad of it all when we get home, for we're going to have a bully trip." How much lighter my pack felt the next day, when I recalled his words of encouragement! How we looked and looked for Seal

Lake, but never found it. It lay hidden among those hills that were away to the northward of us, with its waters as placid and beautiful as they were to-day when we passed through it. I had never seen Michikamau. Was I destined to see it now?

The fire burned low. Only a few glowing coals remained, and as they blackened my picture dissolved. The aurora, like a hundred searchlights, was whipping across the sky. The forest with its hidden mysteries lay dark beneath. A deep, impenetrable silence brooded over all. The vast, indescribable loneliness of the wilderness possessed my soul. I tried to shake off the feeling of desolation as I went to my bed of boughs.

To-morrow a new stage of our journey would begin. It was ho for Michikamau!

Chapter 9: We Lose the Trail

Saturday morning, August fifth, broke with a radiance and a glory seldom equaled even in that land of glorious sunrises and sunsets. A flame of red and orange in the east ushered in the rising sun, not a cloud marred the azure of the heavens, the moss was white with frost, and the crisp, clear atmosphere sweet with the scent of the new day. Labrador was in her most amiable mood, displaying to the best advantage her peculiar charms and beauties.

While we ate a hurried breakfast of corn-meal mush, boiled fat pork and tea, and broke camp, Michikamau was the subject of our conversation, for now it was ho for the big lake! A rapid advance was expected upon the river, and the trail above, where it left the Nascaupee to avoid the rapids which the Indians had told us about, would probably be found without trouble. So this new stage of our journey was begun with something of the enthusiasm that we had felt the day we left Tom Blake's cabin and started up Grand Lake.

We had gone but a mile when Pete drew his paddle from the water and pointed with it at a narrow, sandy beach ahead, above which rose a steep bank. Almost at the same instant I saw the object of his interests--a buck caribou asleep on the sand. The wind was blowing toward the river, and maintaining absolute silence, we landed below a bend that hid us from the caribou. Fresh meat was in sight and we must have it, for we were hungry now for venison. To cover the retreat of the animal should it take alarm, Pete was to go on the top of the bank above it, Easton to take a stand opposite it and I a little below it. We crawled to our positions with the greatest care; but the caribou was alert. The shore breeze carried to it the scent of danger, and almost before we knew, that we were discovered it was on its feet and away. For a fraction of a second I had one glimpse of the animal through the brush. Pete did not see it when it started, but heard it running up the shore, and away be started in that direction, running and leaping recklessly over the fallen tree trunks. Presently the caribou turned from the river and showed itself on the burned plateau above, two hundred yards from Pete. The Indian halted for a moment and fired--then fired again. I hastened up and came upon Pete standing by the prostrate caribou and grinning from ear to ear.

The carcass was quickly skinned and the meat stripped from the bones and carried to the canoe. Here on the shore we made a fire, broiled some thick luscious steaks, roasted some marrow bones and made tea. All the bones except the marrow bones of the legs were abandoned as an unnecessary weight. Pete broke a hole through one of the shoulder blades and stuck it on a limb of a tree above the reach of animals. That, you know, insures further good luck in hunting. It is a sort of offering to the Manitou. We took the skin with us. "Maybe we need him for something," said Pete. "Clean and smoke him nice, me; maybe mend clothes with him."

The larger pieces of our venison were to be roasted when we halted in the evening. We could not dally now, and I chose this method of preserving the meat, rather than "jerk" it (that is, dry it in the open air over a smoky fire), which would have necessitated a halt of three or four days.

Within three hours after we had first seen the caribou we were on our way again. The river up which we were passing was from two to four hundred yards in width, and with the exception of an occasional rock, had a gravelly bottom, and the banks were generally low and gravelly. A little distance back ridges of low hills paralleled the stream, and on the south side behind the lower ridge was a higher one of rough hills; but none of them with an elevation above the valley of more than three hundred feet. The country had been burned on both sides of the river and there was little new growth to hide the dead trees.

Twenty-five miles above Seal Lake we encountered a rapid which necessitated a mile and a half portage around it. Where we landed to make the portage I noticed along the edge of the sandy beach a black band about two feet in width. I thought at first that the water had discolored the sand, but upon a closer examination discovered that it was nothing more nor less than myriads of our black fly pests that had lost their lives in the water and been washed ashore.

We had much rain and progress was slow and difficult in the face of a strong wind and current. Seven or eight miles above the rapid around which we had portaged we passed into a large expansion of the river which the Indians at Northwest River Post had told us to look for, and which they called Wuchusknipi (Big Muskrat) Lake.

High gravelly banks, rising in terraces sometimes fully fifty feet above the water's edge, had now become the feature of the stream. The current increased in strength, and only for short distances above Wuchusknipi, where the river occasionally broadened, were we able to paddle. The tracking lines were brought into service, one man hauling each canoe, while the others, wading in the water, or walking on the bank with poles where the stream was too deep to wade, kept the canoes straight in the current and clear of the shore. Once when it became necessary to cross a wide place in the river a squall struck us, and Richards and Stanton in the smaller canoe were nearly swamped. The strong head wind precluded paddling, even when the current would otherwise have permitted it.

Finally the sky cleared and the wind ceased to blow; but with the calm came a cause for disquietude. A light smoke had settled in the valley and the air held the odor of it, suggesting a forest fire somewhere above. This would mean retreat, if not disaster, for when these fires once start, rivers and lakes prove small obstacles in their path. From a view-point on the hills no dense smoke could be discovered, only the light haze that we had seen and smelled in the valley, and we therefore decided that the gale that had blown for several days from the northwest may have carried it for a long distance, even from the district far west of Michikamau, and that at any rate there was no cause for immediate alarm.

The ridges with an increasing altitude were crowding in upon us more closely. Once when we stopped to portage around a low fall we climbed some of the hills that were near at hand that we might obtain a better knowledge of the topography of the country than could be had from the confined river valley. Away to the northwest we found the country to be much more rugged than the district we had recently passed through. Observations showed us that the highest of the hills we were on had an elevation of six hundred feet above the river. We had but a single day of fine weather and then a fog came so thick that we could not see the opposite banks of the Nascaupee, and after it a cold rain set in which made our work in the icy current doubly hard. One morning I slipped on a boulder in the river and strained my side, and for me the remainder of the day was very trying. That evening we reached a little group of three or four islands, where the Nascaupee was wide and shallow, but just above the islands it narrowed down again and a low fall occurred. Not far from the fall a small river tumbled down over the rocks a sheer thirty feet, and emptied into the Nascaupee. Since leaving Seal Lake we had passed two rivers flowing in from the north, and this was the second one coming from the south, marking the point on the Indian map where we were to look for the portage trail leading to the northward. Therefore a halt was made and camp was pitched.

During the night the weather cleared, and Pete, Richards and Easton were dispatched in the morning to scout the country to the northward in search of the trail and signs of Indians. The ligaments of my side were very stiff and sore from the strain they received the previous day, and I remained in camp with Stanton to write up my records, take an inventory of our food supply, and consider plans for the future.

It was August twelfth. How far we had still to go before reaching Michikamau was uncertain, but, in view of our experiences below Seal Lake and the difficulties met with in finding and following the old Indian trail there, our progress would now, for a time at least, if we traveled the portage route, be slower than on the river where we had done fairly well. True, our outfit was much lighter than it had been in the beginning, and we were in better shape for packing and were able to carry heavier loads. Still we must make two trips over every portage, and that meant, for every five miles of advance, fifteen miles of walking and ten of those miles with packs on our backs. Had we not better, therefore, abandon the further attempt to locate the trail and, instead, follow the river which was beyond doubt the quicker and the easier route? My inclinations rebelled against this course. One of the objects of the expedition, for it was one of the things that Hubbard had planned to do, was to locate the old trail, if possible. To abandon the search for it now, and to follow the easier route, seemed to me a surrender.

On the other hand, should we not find game or fish and have delays scouting for the trail, it would be necessary to go on short rations before reaching Michikamau, for enough food must be held back to take us out of the country in safety.

In my present consideration of the situation it seemed to me highly improbable that we could reach George River Post in season to connect with the Hudson's Bay Company's steamer Pelican, which touches there to land supplies about the middle of September, and that is the only steamer that ever visits that Post. Not to connect with the Pelican would, therefore, mean imprisonment in the north for an entire year, or a return around the coast by dog train in winter. The former of these alternatives was out of the question; the latter would be impossible with an encumbrance of four men, for dog teams and drivers in the early winter are usually all away to the hunting grounds and hard to engage. I therefore concluded that but one course was open to me. Three of the men must be sent back and with a single companion I would push on to Ungava. This, then, was the line of action I decided upon.

Toward evening gathering clouds augured an early renewal of the storm, and Stanton and I had just put up the stove in the tent in anticipation of it when Pete and Easton, the latter thoroughly fagged out, came into camp.

"Well, Pete," I asked, "what luck?"

"Find trail all right," he answered. "Can't follow him easy. Long carry. First lake far, maybe eleven, twelve mile. Little ponds not much good for canoe. Trail old. Not used long time. All time go up hill."

"Where's Richards?" I inquired, noticing his absence.

"Left us about four miles back to take a short cut to the river and follow it down to camp," said Easton. "He thought you might want to know how it looked above, and perhaps keep on that way instead of tackling the portage, for the trail's going to be mighty hard. It looks as though the river would be better."

We waited until near dark for Richards, but he did not come.

Then we ate our supper without him.

The rain grew into a downpour and darkness came, but no Richards, and at length I became alarmed for his safety. I pushed back the tent flaps and peered out into the pitchy darkness and pouring rain.

"He'll never get in to-night," I remarked. "No," said someone, "and he'll have a hard time of it out there in the rain." There was nothing to do but wait. Pete rummaged in his bag and produced a candle (we had a dozen in our outfit), sharpened one end of a stick, split the other end for two or three inches down, forced open the split end and set the candle in it and stuck the sharpened end in the ground, all the while working in the dark. Then he lit the candle.

I do not know how long we had been sitting by the candle light and putting forth all sorts of conjectures about Richards and his uncomfortable position in the bush without cover and the probable reasons for his failure to return, when the tent front opened and in he came, as wet as though he had been in the river.

"Well, Richards," I asked, when he was comfortably settled at his meal, "what do you think of the river?"

"The river!" he paused between mouthfuls to exclaim, "that's the only thing within twenty miles that I didn't see. I've been looking for it for four hours, but it kept changing its location and I never found it till I struck camp just now."

"Now, boys," said I, when all the pipes were going, "I've something to say to you. Up to this time we've had no real hardships to meet. We've had hard work, and it's been most trying at times, but there's always hardship and trial to endure upon any journey in the bush. If we go on we shall have hardships, and perhaps, some pretty severe ones. There'll soon be sleet and snow in the air, and cold days and shivery nights, and the portages will be long and hard. On the whole, there's been plenty to eat--not what we would have had at home, perhaps, but good, wholesome grub--and we're all in better condition and stronger than when we started, but flour and pork are getting low, lentils and corn meal are nearly gone, and short rations, with hungry days, are soon to come if we don't strike game, and you know how uncertain that is. I cannot say what is before us, and I'm not going to drag you fellows into trouble. I'm going to ask for one volunteer to go on with me to Ungava with the small canoe, and let the rest return from here with the other canoe and what grub they need to take them out. Who wants to go home?"

It came to them like a shock. Outside, the wind howled through the trees and dashed the rain spitefully against the tent. The water dripped through on us, and the candle flickered and sputtered and almost went out. In the weird light I could see the faces of the men work with emotion. For a moment no one spoke. Finally Richards, in a tone of reproach that made me feel sorry for the very suggestion, asked: "Do you think there's a quitter here?"

The loyalty and grit of the men touched my heart. Not one of them would think of leaving me. Nothing but a positive order would have turned them back, and I decided to postpone our parting until we reached Michikaumau at least, if it could be postponed so long consistently with safety.

The next day was Sunday, and it was spent in rest and in preparation for our advance up the trail. The weather was damp and cheerless, with rain falling intermittently throughout the day.

To cover a possible retreat a cache was made near our camp of thirty pounds of pemmican in tin cans and forty-five pounds of flour and some tea in a waterproof bag. A hole was dug in the ground and the provisions were deposited in it, then covered with stones as a protection from animals.

By Monday morning the storm had gained new strength, and steadily and pitilessly the rain fell, accompanied by a cold, northwest wind.

What narrowly escaped being a serious accident occurred when we halted that day for dinner. Easton was cutting firewood, when suddenly he dropped the ax he was using with the exclamation "That fixes me!" He had given himself what looked at first like an ugly cut near the shin bone. Fortunately, however, upon examination, it proved to be only a flesh wound and not sufficiently severe to interfere with his traveling. Stanton dressed the cut. Our adhesive plaster we found had become useless by exposure and electrician's tape was substituted for it to draw the flesh together.

On the evening of the second day after leaving the Nascaupee, our tent was pitched upon the site of an extensive but ancient Indian camp beside a mile-long lake, four hundred and fifty feet above the river. Five ponds had been passed en route, but all of them so small it was scarcely worthwhile floating the canoe in any of them.

In these two days we had covered but eleven miles, but during the whole time the wind had driven the rain in sweeping gusts into our faces and made it impossible for a man, single-handed, to portage a canoe. Thus, with two men to carry each canoe we had been compelled to make three loads of our outfit, and this meant fifty-five miles actual walking, and thirty-three miles of this distance with packs on our backs. The weather conditions had made the work more than hard-- it was heartrending--as we toiled over naked hills, across marshes and moraines, or through dripping brush and timber land.

A beautiful afternoon, two days later, found us paddling down the first lake worthy of mention since leaving the Nascaupee River. The azure sky overhead shaded to a pearly blue at the horizon, with a fleecy cloud or two floating lazily across its face. The atmosphere was perfect in its purity, and only the sound of screeching gulls and the dip of our paddles disturbed the quiet of the wilderness. Lake Bibiquasin, as we shall call it, was five miles in length and nestled between ridges of low, moss-covered hills. It lay in a southeasterly and northwesterly direction, and rested upon the summit of a sub-sidiary divide that we had been gradually ascending. A creek ran out of its northwesterly end, flowing in that direction.

Until now we had found the trail with little difficulty, but here we were baffled. A search in the afternoon failed to uncover it, and we were forced to halt, perplexed again as to our course. Camp was pitched in a grove of spruces at the lower end of the lake. Not far from us was an old hunting camp which Pete said was "most hundred years old," and he was not far wrong in his estimate, for the frames upon which the Indians had stretched skins and the tepee poles crumbled to pieces when we touched them.

Strange to say, not a fish of any description had been seen for several days and not one could be induced to rise to fly or bait, and our net was always empty now. Game, too, was scarce. There were no fresh caribou tracks this side of the

Nascaupee River, and but one duck and one spruce partridge had been killed. The last bit of our venison was eaten the day before. It was pretty badly spoiled and turning a little green in color, but Pete washed it well several times and we all avoided the lee side of the kettle while it was cooking. It was pronounced "not so bad."

Another day was lost on Lake Bibiquasin in an ineffectual hunt for the trail. I scouted alone all day and in my wanderings came upon the first ptarmigans of the trip and shot one of them with my rifle. The others flew away. They wore their mottled summer coat, as it was still too early for them to don their pure white dress of winter.

During my scouting trip I also discovered the first ripe bake-apple berries we had seen. This is a salmon-colored berry resembling in size and shape the raspberry, and grows on a low plant like the strawberry.

On Saturday morning, August nineteenth, the temperature was four degrees below the freezing point, and the ground was stiff with frost. In a further search on the north side of the lake opposite our camp we found an old blaze and a trail leading from it along a ridge and through marshes to a small lake. This was the only trail that we could find anywhere, so we decided to follow it, though it did not bear all the earmarks of the portage trail we had been tracing--it was decidedly more ancient. We started our work with a will. It was a hard portage and we sometimes sank knee deep into the marsh and got mired frequently, but finally reached the lake.

Indian signs now completely disappeared. Down the lake, where a creek flowed out, was a bare hill, and Pete and I climbed it. From its summit we could easily locate the creek taking a turn to the north and then to the northeast and, finally, flowing into one of a series of lakes extending in an easterly and westerly direction. The land was comparatively flat to the eastward and the lakes no doubt fed a river flowing out of that end, probably one of those that we had noted as joining the Nascaupee on its north side. To the north of these lakes were high, rugged ridges. It was possible there was an opening in the hills to the westward, where they seemed lower; we could not tell from where we were, but we determined to portage along the creek into the lakes with that hope.

Again the smoke of a forest fire hung in the valleys and over the hills, and the air was heavy with the smell of it, which revived the former uneasiness, but by the next day every trace of it had disappeared.

Another day found us afloat upon the first of the lakes. Several short carries across necks of land took us from this lake into the one which Pete and I had seen extending back to the ridges to the westward, and which we shall call Lake Desolation.

On the northern shore of Lake Desolation we stopped to climb a mountain. A decided change in the features of the country had taken place since leaving Lake Bibiquasin, and the low moss-covered hills had given place to rough mountains of bare rock. To the northward from where we stood nothing but higher mountains of similar formation met our view--a great, rolling vista of bare, desolate rocks. To the westward the country was not, perhaps, so rough, though there, too, in the far distance could be discerned the tops of rugged hills breaking the line of the horizon. Through a valley in that direction was distinguishable, with a considerable interval between them, a string of small lakes or ponds. This valley led up from the western end of Lake Desolation, and there was no other possible place for the trail to leave the lake. The valley was the only opening.

Our mountain climbing had consumed a good part of an afternoon, and it was evening when finally we reached the western end of the lake and pitched our camp near a creek flowing in. As we paddled we tried our trolls, but were not rewarded with a single strike. When camp was made the net was stretched across the creek's mouth and we tried our rods in the stream for trout, but our efforts were useless. No fish were caught.

The prospect for game had not improved, in fact was growing steadily worse. We were now in a country that had been desolated by a forest fire within four or five years. The moss under foot had not renewed itself and where any of it remained at all, it was charred and black. The trees were dead and the land harbored almost no life. It seemed to me that even the fish had been scalded out of the water and the streams had never restocked themselves.

A thorough search was made for Indian signs, but there were absolutely none. There was nothing to show that any human being had ever been here before us. Back on Lake Bibiquasin we had lost the trail and now on Lake Desolation we were far and hopelessly astray, with only the compass to guide us.

After supper the men sat around the camp fire, smoking and talking of their friends at home, while I walked alone by the lake shore. It was a wild scene that lay before me--the aurora, with its waves of changing color flashing weirdly as they swept and lighted the sky, the dead trees everywhere like skeletons gray and gaunt, the blazing camp fire in the foreground, with the figures lying about it and the little white tent in the background. Somewhere hidden in the depths of that vast and silent wilderness to the westward lay Michikamau.

There was no mark on the face of the earth to direct us on our road. We must blaze a new trail up that valley and over those ridges that looked so dark and forbidding in the uncertain light of the aurora. We must find Michikamau.

Chapter 10: We See Michikamau

"It's no use, Pete. You may as well go back to your blankets."

It was the morning of the second day after reaching the lake which we named Desolation. We had portaged through a valley and over a low ridge to the shores of a pond, out of which a small stream ran to the southeast. The country was devastated by fire and to the last degree inhospitable. Not a green shrub over two feet in height was to be seen, the trees were dead and blackened; not even the customary moss covered the naked earth, and loose boulders were scattered everywhere about.

There was no fixed trail now to look for or to guide us, but by keeping a general westerly course, we knew that we must, sooner or later, reach Michikamau. Rough, irregular ridges blocked our path and it was necessary to look ahead that we might not become tangled up amongst them. One hill, higher than the others, a solitary bailiff that guarded the wilderness beyond, was to have been climbed this morning, but when Pete and I at daybreak came out of the tent we were met by driving rain and dashes of sleet that cut our faces, and a mist hung over the earth so thick we could not even see across the tiny lake at our feet. I looked longingly into the storm and mist in the direction in which I knew the big hill lay, and realized the hopelessness and foolhardiness of attempting to reach it.

"It's no use, Pete," I continued, "to try to scout in this storm. You could see nothing from the hill if you reached it, and the chances are, with every landmark hidden, you couldn't find the tent again. I don't want to lose you yet. Go back and sleep."

Later in the morning to my great relief the weather cleared, and Richards and Pete were at once dispatched to scout. We who remained "at home," as we called our camp, found plenty of work to keep us occupied. The bushes had ravaged our clothing to such an extent that some of us were pretty ragged, and every halt was taken advantage of to make much needed repairs.

It was nearly dark when Richards and Pete came back. They had reached the high hill and from its summit saw, some distance to the westward, long stretches of water reaching far away to the hills in that direction. A portage of several miles in which some small lakes occurred would take us, they said, into a large lake. Beyond this they could not see.

Pete brought back with him a hatful of ripe currants which he stewed and which proved a very welcome addition to our supper of corn-meal mush.

The report of water ahead made us happy. It was now August twenty- third. If we could reach Michikamau by September first that should give me ample time, I believed, to reach the George River before the caribou migration would take place.

The following morning we started forward with a will, and with many little lakes to cross and short portages between them, we made fairly good progress, and each lake took us one step higher on the plateau.

The character of the country was changing, too. The naked land and rocks and dead trees gave way to a forest of green spruce, and the ground was again covered with a thick carpet of white caribou moss.

We were catching no fish, however, although our efforts to lure them to the hook or entangle them in the net were never relinquished. Pork was a luxury, and no baker ever produced anything half so dainty and delicious as our squaw bread. A strict distribution of rations was maintained, and when the pork was fried, Pete, with a spoon, dished out the grease into the five plates in equal shares. Into this the quarter loaf ration of bread was broken and the mixture eaten to the last morsel. Sometimes the men drank the warm pork grease clear. Finally it became so precious that they licked their plates after scraping them with their spoons, and the longing eyes that were cast at the frying pan made me fear that some time a raid would be made on that.

One day, an owl was shot and went into the pot to keep company with a couple of partridges. Pete demurred. "Owl eat mice," said he. "Not good man eat him."

"You can count me out on owl, too," Richards volunteered.

"Oh! they're all right," I assured them. "The Labrador people always eat them and you'll find them very nice."

"Not me. Owl eat mice," Pete insisted.

"Well," I suggested, "possibly we'll be eating mice, too, before we get home, and it's a good way to begin by eating owl--for then the mice won't seem so bad when we have to eat them."

Stanton took charge of the kettle and dished out the rations that night.

"Partridge is good enough for me," said Richards, fearing that Stanton might forget his prejudice against owl.

"Me, too," echoed Pete.

"I'll take owl," said I.

Easton said nothing.

After we had eaten, Stanton asked: "How'd you like the partridge, Richards?"

"It was fine," said he. "Guess it was a piece of a young one you gave me, for it wasn't as tough as they usually are."

"Maybe it was young, but that partridge was owl." "I'll be darned!" exclaimed Richards. His face was a study for a moment, then he laughed. "If that was owl they're all right and I'm a convert. I'll eat all I can get after this."

After leaving Lake Desolation the owls had begun to come to us, and Richards was one of the best owl hunters of the party. At first one or two a day were killed, but now whenever we halted an owl would fly into a tree and twitter, and, with a very wise appearance, proceed to look us over as though he wanted to find out what we were up to anyway, for these owls were very inquisitive fellows. He immediately became a candidate for our pot, and as many as six were shot in one day. The men called them the "manna of the Labrador wilderness." Pete's disinclination to eat them was quickly forgotten, for hunger is a wonderful killer of prejudices, and he was as keen for them now as any of us.

An occasional partridge was killed and now and again a black duck or two helped out our short ration, but the owls were our mainstay. We did not have enough to satisfy the appetites of five hungry men, however; still we did fairly well.

The days were growing perceptibly shorter with each sunset, and the nights were getting chilly. On the night of August twenty-fifth, the thermometer registered a minimum temperature of twenty-five degrees above zero, and on the twenty-sixth of August, forty-eight degrees was the maximum at midday.

During the forenoon of that day we reached the largest of the lakes that the scouting party had seen three days before, and further scouting was now necessary. At the western end of the lake, about two miles from where we entered, a hill offered itself as a point from which to view the country beyond, and here we camped.

We were now out of the burned district and the scant growth of timber was apparently the original growth, though none of the trees was more than eight inches or so in diameter. In connection with this it might be of interest to note here the fact that the timber line ended at an elevation of two hundred and seventy-five feet above the lake. The hill was four hundred feet high and there was not a vestige of vegetation on its summit. The top of the hill was strewn with boulders, large and small, lying loose upon the clean, storm-scoured bed rock, just as the glaciers had left them.

What a view we had! To the northwest, to the west, and to the southwest, for fifty miles in any direction was a network of lakes, and the country was as level as a table. The men called it "the plain of a thousand lakes," and this describes it well. To the far west a line of blue hills extending to the northwest and southeast cut off our view beyond. They were low, with but one high, conical peak standing out as a landmark. Another ridge at right angles to this one ran to the eastward, bounding the lakes on that side. I examined them carefully through my binoculars and discovered a long line of water, like a silver thread, following the ridge running eastward, and decided that this must be the Nascaupee River, though later I was convinced that I was mistaken and that the river lay to the southward of the ridge. To the cast and north of our hill was an expanse of rolling, desolate wilderness. Carefully I examined with my glass the great plain of lakes, hoping that I might discover the smoke of a wigwam fire or some other sign of life, but none was to be seen. It was as still and dead as the day it was created. It was a solemn, awe-inspiring scene, impressive beyond description, and one that I shall not soon forget.

We outlined as carefully as possible the course that we should follow through the maze of lakes, with the round peak as our objective point, for just south of it there seemed to be an opening through the ridge: beyond which we hoped lay Michikamau.

The next day we portaged through a marsh and into the lake country and made some progress, portaging from lake to lake across swampy and marshy necks. It was Sunday, but we did not realize it until our day's work was finished and we were snug in camp in the evening.

Monday's dawn brought with it a day of superb loveliness. The sky was cloudless, the earth was white with hoarfrost, the atmosphere was crisp and cool, and we took deep breaths of it that sent the blood tingling through our veins. It was a day that makes one love life.

Through small lakes and short portages we worked until afternoon and then--hurrah! we were on big water again. Thirty or forty miles in length the lake stretched off to the westward to carry us on our way. It was choked in places with many fir-topped islands, and the channels in and out amongst these islands were innumerable, so Pete called it Lake Kasheshebogamog, which in his language means "Lake of Many Channels."

As we paddled I dropped a troll and before we stopped for the night landed a seven-pound namaycush, and another large one broke a troll. The "Land of God's Curse" was behind us. We were with the fish again, and caribou and wolf tracks were seen.

The next day found us on our way early. A fine wind sent us spinning before it and at the same time kept us busy with a rough sea that was running on the wide, open lake when we were away from the shelter of the islands. At one o'clock we boiled the kettle at the foot of a low sand ridge, and upon climbing the ridge we found it covered with a mass of ripe blueberries. We ate our fill and picked some to carry with us.

At three o'clock we were brought up sharply at the end of the water with no visible outlet. The nature of the lake and the lateness of the season made it impracticable to turn back and look in other channels for the connection with western waters. Former experience had taught me that we might paddle around for a week before we found it, for these were big waters. Five miles ahead was the high, round peak that we were aiming for, and I had every confidence that from its top Michikamau could be seen and a way to reach the big lake. I decided that it must be climbed the next morning, and selected Pete and Easton for the work. A fall the day before had given me a stiff knee, and it was a bitter disappointment that I could not go myself, for I was nervously anxious for a first view of Michikamau. However, I realized that it was unwise to attempt the journey, and I must stay behind.

That night Stanton made two roly-polies of the blueberries we picked in the afternoon, boiling them in specimen bags, and we used the last of our sugar for sauce. This, with coffee, followed a good supper of boiled partridge and owl. It was like the old days when I was with Hubbard. We were making good progress, our hopes ran high, and we must feast. Pete's laughs, and songs and jokes added to our merriment. Rain came, but we did not mind that. We sat by a big, blazing fire and ate and enjoyed ourselves in spite of it. Then we went to the tent to smoke and every one pronounced it the best night in weeks.

On Wednesday rain poured down at the usual rising time and the men were delayed in starting, for we were in a place where scouting in thick weather was dangerous. It was the morning of the famous eclipse, but we had forgotten the fact. The rain had fallen away to a drizzle and we were eating a late breakfast when the darkness came. It did not last long, and then the rain stopped, though the sky was still overcast. Shortly after breakfast Pete and Easton left us. I gave Pete a new corncob pipe as he was leaving. When he put it in his pocket he said, "I smoke him when I see Michikaman, when I climb hill, if Michikamau there. Sit down, me, look at big water, feel good then. Smoke pipe, me, and call hill Corncob Hill."

"All right," said I, laughing at Pete's fancy. "I hope the hill will have a name to-day."

It was really a day of anxiety for me, for if Michikamau were not visible from the mountain top with the wide view of country that it must offer, then we were too far away from the lake to hope to reach it.

A mile from camp, Richards discovered a good-sized river flowing in from the northwest and set the net in it. Then he and Stanton paddled up the river a mile and a half to another lake, but did not explore it farther.

With what impatience I awaited the return of Pete and Easton can be imagined, and when, near dusk, I saw them coming I almost dreaded to hear their report, for what if they had not seen Michikamau?

But they had seen Michikamau. When Pete was within talking distance of me, he shouted exultantly, "We see him! We see him! We see Michikamau!"

Chapter 11: The Parting at Michikamau

Pete and Easton had taken their course through small, shallow, rocky lakes until they neared the base of the round hill. Here the canoe was left, and up the steep side of the hill they climbed. "When we most up," Pete told me afterward, "I stop and look at Easton. My heart beat fast. I most afraid to look. Maybe Michikamau not there. Maybe I see only hills. Then I feel bad. Make me feel bad come back and tell you Michikamau not there. I see you look sorry when I tell you that. Then I think if Michikamau there you feel very good. I must know quick. I run. I run fast. Hill very steep. I do not care. I must know soon as I can, and I run. I shut my eyes just once, afraid to look. Then I open them and look. Very close I see when I open my eyes much water. Big water. So big I see no land when I look one way; just water. Very wide too, that water. I know I see Michikamau. My heart beat easy and I feel very glad. I almost cry. I remember corncob pipe you give me, and what I tell you. I take pipe out my pocket. I fill him, and light him. Then I sit on rock and smoke. All the time I look at Michikamau. I feel good and I say, 'This we call Corncob Hill.'"

And so we were all made glad and the conical peak had a name.

Pete told me that we should have to cut the ridge to the south of Corncob Hill, taking a rather wide detour to reach the place. A chain of lakes would help us, but some long portages were necessary and it would require several days' hard work. This we did not mind now. We were only anxious to dip our paddles into the waters of the big lake. At last Michikamau, which I had so longed to see through two summers of hardship in the Labrador wilds, was near, and I could hope to be rewarded with a look at it within the week.

But with the joy of it there was also a sadness, for I must part from three of my loyal companions. The condition of our commissariat and the cold weather that was beginning to be felt made it imperative that the men be sent back from the big lake.

The possibility of this contingency had been foreseen by me before leaving New York, and I had mentioned it at that time. Easton had asked me then, if the situation would permit of it, to consider him as a candidate to go through with me to Ungava. When the matter had been suggested at the last camp on the Nascaupee River be had again earnestly solicited me to choose him as my companion, and upon several subsequent occasions had mentioned it. Richards was the logical man for me to choose, for he had had experience in rapids, and could also render me valuable assistance in the scientific work that the others were not fitted for. He was exceedingly anxious to continue the journey, but his university duties demanded his presence in New York in the winter, and I had promised his people that he should return home in the autumn. This made it out of the question to keep him with me, and it was a great disappointment to both of us. That I might feel better assured of the safety of the returning men, I decided to send Pete back with them to act as their guide. Stanton, too, wished to go on, but Easton had spoken first, so I decided to give him the opportunity to go with me to Ungava, as my sole companion.

That night, after the others had gone to bed, we two sat late by the camp fire and talked the matter over. "It's a dangerous undertaking, Easton," I said, "and I want you to understand thoroughly what you're going into. Before we reach the George River Post we shall have over four hundred miles of territory to traverse. We may have trouble in locating the George River, and when we do find it there will be heavy rapids to face, and its whole course will be filled with perils. If any accident happens to either of us we shall be in a bad fix. For that reason it's always particularly dangerous for less than three men to travel in a country like this. Then there's the winter trip with dogs. Every year natives are caught in storms, and some of them perish. We shall be exposed to the perils and hardships of one of the longest dog trips ever made in a single season, and we shall be traveling the whole winter. I want you to understand this."

"I do understand it," he answered, "and I'm ready for it. I want to go on."

And so it was finally settled.

It was not easy for me to tell the men that the time had come when we must part, for I realized how hard it would be for them to turn back. The next morning after breakfast, I asked them to remain by the fire and light their pipes. Then I told them. Richards' eyes filled with tears. Stanton at first said he would not turn back without me, but finally agreed with me that it was best he should. Pete urged me to let him go on. Later he stole quietly into the tent, where I was alone writing, and without a word sat opposite me, looking very woe-begone. After awhile he spoke: "Today I feel very sad. I forget to smoke. My pipe go out and I do not light it. I think all time of you. Very lonely, me. Very bad to leave you."

Here he nearly broke down, and for a little while he could not speak. When he could control himself he continued:

"Seems like I take four men in bush, lose two. Very bad, that. Don't know how I see your sisters. I go home well. They ask me, 'Where my brother?' I don't know. I say nothing. Maybe you die in rapids. Maybe you starve. I don't know. I say nothing. Your sisters cry." Then his tone changed from brokenhearted dejection to one of eager pleading:

"Wish you let me go with you. Short grub, maybe. I hunt. Much danger; don't care, me. Don't care what danger. Don't care if grub short. Maybe you don't find portage. Maybe not find river. That bad. I find him. I take you through. I bring you back safe to your sisters. Then I speak to them and they say I do right."

It was hard to withstand Pete's pleadings, but my duty was plain, and I said:

"No, Pete. I'd like to take you through, but I've got to send you back to see the others safely out. Tell my sisters I'm safe. Tell everybody we're safe. I'm sure we'll get through all right. We'll do our best, and trust to God for the rest, so don't worry. We'll be all right."

"I never think you do this," said he. "I don't think you leave me this way." After a pause be continued, "If grub short, come back. Don't wait too long. If you find Indian, then you all right. He help you. You short grub, don't find Indian, that bad. Don't wait till grub all gone. Come back."

Pete did not sing that day, and he did not smoke. He was very sad and quiet.

We spent the day in assorting and dividing the outfit, the men making a cache of everything that they would not need until their return, that we might not be impeded in our progress to Michikamau. They would get their things on their way back. Eight days, Pete said, would see them from this point to the cache we had made on the Nascaupee, and only eight days' rations would they accept for the journey. They were more than liberal. Richards insisted that I take a new Pontiac shirt that he had reserved for the cold weather, and Pete gave me a new pair of larigans. They deprived themselves that we might be comfortable. Easton and I were to have the tent, the others would use the tarpaulin for a wigwam shelter; each party would have two axes, and the other things were divided as best we could. Richards presented us with a package that we were not to open until the sixteenth of September--his birthday. It was a special treat of some kind.

Some whitefish, suckers and one big pike were taken out of the net, which was also left for them to pick up upon their return. A school of large pike had torn great holes in it, but it was still useful.

We were a sorrowful group that gathered around the fire that night. The evening was raw. A cold north wind soughed wearily through the fir tops. Black patches of clouds cast a gloom over everything, and there was a vast indefiniteness to the dark spruce forest around us. I took a flashlight picture of the men around the fire. Then we sat awhile and talked, and finally went to our blankets in the chilly tent.

September came with a leaden sky and cold wind, but the clouds were soon dispelled, and the sun came bright and warm. Our progress was good, though we had several portages to make. On September second, at noon, we left the larger canoe for the men to get on their way back, and continued with the eighteen-foot canoe, which, with its load of outfit and five men, was very deep in the water, but no wind blew and the water was calm.

Here the character of the lakes changed. The waters were deep and black, the shores were steep and rocky, and some labradorite was seen. One small, curious island, evidently of iron, though we did not stop to examine it, took the form of a great head sticking above the water, with the tops of the shoulders visible.

Sunday, September third, was a memorable day, a day that I shall never forget while I live. The morning came with all the glories of a northern sunrise, and the weather was perfect. After two short portages and two small lakes were crossed, Pete said, "Now we make last portage and we reach Michikamau." It was not a long portage--a half mile, perhaps. We passed through a thick-grown defile, Pete ahead, and I close behind him. Presently we broke through the bush and there before us was the lake. We threw down our packs by the water's edge. We had reached Michikamau. I stood uncovered as I looked over the broad, far-reaching waters of the great lake. I cannot describe my emotions. I was living over again that beautiful September day two years before when Hubbard had told me with so much joy that he had seen the big lake--that Michikamau lay just beyond the ridge. Now I was on its very shores--the shores of the lake that we had so longed to reach. How well I remembered those weary wind-bound days, and the awful weeks that followed. It was like the recollection of a horrid dream--his dear, wan face, our kiss and embrace, my going forth into the storm and the eternity of horrors that was crowded into days. Pete, I think, understood, for he had heard the story. He stood for a moment in silence, then he fashioned his hat brim into a cup, and dipping some water handed it to me. "You reach Michikamau at last. Drink Michikamau water before others come." I drank reverently from the hat. Then the others joined us and we all stood for a little with bowed uncovered beads, on the shore.

Our camp was pitched on an elevated, rocky point a few hundred yards farther up--the last camp that we were to have together, and the forty-sixth since leaving Northwest River. We had made over half a hundred portages, and traveled about three hundred and twenty-five miles.

The afternoon was occupied in writing letters and telegrams to the home folks, for Richards to take out with him; after which we divided the food. Easton and I were to take with us seventy-eight pounds of pemmican, twelve pounds of pea meal, seven pounds of pork, some beef extract, eight pounds of flour, one cup of corn meal, a small quantity of desiccated vegetables, one pound of coffee, two pounds of tea, some salt and crystallose. Richards gave us nearly all of his tobacco, and Pete kept but two plugs for himself.

Toward evening we gathered about our fire, and talked of our parting and of the time when we should meet again. Every remaining moment we had of each other's company was precious to us now.

The day had been glorious and the night was one of rare beauty. We built a big fire of logs, and by its light I read aloud, in accordance with our custom on Sunday nights, a chapter from the Bible. After this we talked for a while, then sat silent, gazing into the glowing embers of our fire. Finally Pete began singing softly, "Home, Sweet Home" in Indian, and followed it with an old Ojibway song, "I'm Going Far Away, My Heart Is Sore." Then he sang an Indian hymn, "Pray For Me While I Am Gone." When his hymn was finished he said, very reverently, "I going pray for you fellas every day when I say my prayers. I can't pray much without my book, but I do my best. I pray the best I can for you every day." Pete's devotion was sincere, and I thanked him. Stanton sang a solo, and then all joined in "Auld Lang Syne." After this Pete played softly on the harmonica, while we watched the moon drop behind the horizon in the west. The fire burned out and its embers blackened. Then we went to our bed of fragrant spruce boughs, to prepare for the day of our parting.

The morning of September fourth was clear and beautiful and perfect, but in spite of the sunshine and fragrance that filled the air our hearts were heavy when we gathered at our fire to eat the last meal that we should perhaps ever have together.

When we were through, I read from my Bible the fourteenth of John--the chapter that I had read to Hubbard that stormy October morning when we said good-by forever.

The time of our parting had come. I do not think I had fully realized before how close my bronzed, ragged boys had grown to me in our months of constant companionship. A lump came in my throat, and the tears came to the eyes of Richards and Pete, as we grasped each other's hands.

Then we left them. Easton and I dipped our paddles into the water, and our lonely, perilous journey toward the dismal wastes beyond the northern divide was begun. Once I turned to see the three men, with packs on their backs, ascending the knoll back of the place where our camp had been. When I looked again they were gone.

Chapter 12: Over the Northern Divide

Michikamau is approximately between eighty and ninety miles in length, including the unexplored southeast bay, and from eight to twenty-five miles in width. It is surrounded by rugged hills, which reach an elevation of about five hundred feet above the lake. They are generally wooded for perhaps two hundred feet from the base, with black spruce, larch, and an occasional small grove of white birch. Above the timber line their tops are uncovered save by white lichens or stunted shrubs. The western side of the lake is studded with low islands, but its main body is unobstructed. The water is exceedingly clear, and is said by the Indians to have a great depth. The shores are rocky, sometimes formed of massive bed rock in which is found the beautifully colored labradorite; sometimes strewn with loose boulders. Our entrance had been made in a bay several miles north of the point where the Nascaupee River, its outlet, leaves the lake and we kept to the east side as we paddled north.

No artist's imaginative brush ever pictured such gorgeous sunsets and sunrises as Nature painted for us here on the Great Lake of the Indians. Every night the sun went down in a blaze of glory and left behind it all the colors of the spectrum. The dark hills across the lake in the west were silhouetted against a sky of brilliant red which shaded off into banks of orange and amber that reached the azure at the zenith. The waters of the lake took the reflection of the red at the horizon and became a flood of restless blood. The sky colorings during these few days were the finest that I ever saw in Labrador, not only in the evening but in the morning also.

Michikamau has a bad name amongst the Indians for heavy seas, particularly in the autumn months when the northwest gales sometimes blow for weeks at a time without cessation, and the Indians say that they are often held on its shores for long periods by high running seas that no canoe could weather. These were the same winds that held Hubbard and me prisoners for nearly two weeks on the smaller Windbound Lake in 1903, bringing us to the verge of starvation before we were permitted to begin our race for life down the trail toward Northwest River. Fate was kinder now, and but one day's rough water interfered with progress.

Early on the third day after parting from the other men, we found ourselves at the end of Michikamau where a shallow river, in which large boulders were thickly scattered, flowed into it from the north. This was the stream draining Lake Michikamats, the next important point in our journey. Michikamau, it might be explained, means, in the Indian tongue, big water--so big you cannot see the land beyond; Michikamats means a smaller body of water beyond which land may be seen. So somebody has paradoxically defined it "a little big lake."

Barring a single expansion of somewhat more than a mile in length the Michakamats River, which runs through a flat, marshy and uninteresting country, was too shallow to float our canoes, and we were compelled to portage almost its entire length.

In the wide marshes between these two lakes we met the first evidences of the great caribou migration. The ground was tramped like a barnyard, in wide roads, by vast herds of deer, all going to the eastward. There must have been thousands of them in the bands. Most of the hoof marks were not above a day or two old and had all been made since the last rain had fallen, as was evidenced by freshly turned earth and newly tramped vegetation. We saw none of the animals, however, and there were no hills near from which we might hope to sight the herds.

Evidences of life were increasing and game was becoming abundant as we approached the height of land. Some geese and ptarmigans were killed and a good many of both kinds of birds were seen, as well as some ducks. We began to live in plenty now and the twittering owls were permitted to go unmolested.

Lake Michikamats is irregular in shape, about twenty miles long, and, exclusive of its arms, from two to six miles wide. The surrounding country is flat and marshy, with some low, barren hills on the westward side of the lake. The timber growth in the vicinity is sparse and scrubby, consisting of spruce and tamarack. The latter had now taken on its autumnal dress of yellow, and, interspersing the dark green of the spruce, gave an exceedingly beautiful effect to the landscape.

Where we entered Michikamats, at its outlet, the lake is very shallow and filled with boulders that stand high above the water. A quarter of a mile above this point the water deepens, and farther up seems to have a considerable depth, though we did not sound it. The western shore of the upper half is lined with low islands scantily covered with spruce and tamarack.

During two days that we spent here in a thorough exploration of the lake, our camp was pitched on an island at the bottom of a bay that, half way up the lake, ran six miles to the northward. This was selected as the most likely place for the portage trail to leave the lake, as the island had apparently, for a long period, been the regular rendezvous of Indians, not only in summer, but also in winter. Tepee poles of all ages, ranging from those that were old and decayed to freshly cut ones, were numerous. They were much longer and thicker than those used by the Indians south of Michikamau. Here, also, was a well-built log cache, a permanent structure, which was, no doubt, regularly used by hunting parties. Some new snowshoe frames were hanging on the trees to season before being netted with babiche. On the lake shore were some other camping places that had been used within a few months, and at one of them a newly made "sweat hole," where the medicine man had treated the sick. These sweat holes are much in favor with the Labrador Indians, both Mountaineers and Nascaupees. They are about two feet in depth and large enough in circumference for a man to sit in the center, surrounded by a circle of good-sized boulders. Small saplings are bent to form a dome-shaped frame for the top. The invalid is placed in the center of this circle of boulders, which have previously been made very hot, water is poured on them to produce steam, and a blanket thrown over the sapling frame to confine the steam.

The Indians have great faith in this treatment as a cure for almost every malady.

On the mainland opposite the island upon which we were encamped was a barren hill which we climbed, and which commanded a view of a large expanse of country. On the top was a small cairn and several places where fires had been made--no doubt Indian signal fires. The fuel for them must have been carried from the valley below, for not a stick or bush grew on the hill itself. "Signal Hill," as we called it, is the highest elevation for many miles around and a noticeable landmark.

To the northward, at our feet, were two small lakes, and just beyond, trending somewhat to the northwest, was a long lake reaching up through the valley until it was lost in the low hills and sparse growth of trees beyond. Great boulders were strewn indiscriminately everywhere, and the whole country was most barren and desolate. To the south of Michikamats was the stretch of flat swamp land which extended to Michikaman. Petscapiskau, a prominent and rugged peak on the west shore of Michikamau near its upper end, stood out against the distant horizon, a lone sentinel of the wilderness.

The head waters of the George River must now be located. There was nothing to guide me in the search, and the Indians at Northwest River had warned us that we were liable at this point to be led astray by an entanglement of lakes, but I felt certain that any water flowing northward that we might come to, in this longitude, would either be the river itself or a tributary of it, and that some such stream would certainly be found as soon as the divide was crossed.

With this object in view we kept a course nearly due north, passing through four good-sized lakes, until, one afternoon, at the end of a short portage, we reached a narrow, shallow lake lying in an easterly and westerly direction, whose water was very clear and of a bottle- green color, in marked contrast to that of the preceding lakes, which had been of a darker shade.

This peculiarity of the water led me to look carefully for a current when our canoe was launched, and I believed I noticed one. Then I fancied I heard a rapid to the westward. Easton said there was no current and he could not hear a rapid, and to satisfy myself, we paddled toward the sound. We had not gone far when the current became quite perceptible, and just above could be seen the waters of a brook that fed the lake, pouring down through the rocks. We were on the George River at last! Our feelings can be imagined when the full realization of our good fortune came to us, and we turned our canoe to float down on the current of the little stream that was to grow into a mighty river as it carried us on its turbulent bosom toward Ungava Bay.

The course of the stream here was almost due east. The surrounding country continued low and swampy. Tamarack was the chief timber and much of it was straight and fine, with some trees fully twelve inches in diameter at the butt, and fifty feet in height.

A rocky, shallow place in the river that we had to portage brought us into an expansion of considerable size, and here we pitched our first camp on the George River. This was an event that Hubbard had planned and pictured through the weary weeks of hardship on the Susan Valley trail and the long portages across the ranges in his expedition of 1903.

"When we reach the George River, we'll meet the Indians and all will be well," he used to say, and how anxiously we looked forward for that day, which never came.

At the time when he made the suggestion to turn back from Windbound Lake I at first opposed it on the ground that we could probably reach the George River, where game would be found and the Indians would be met with, in much less time than it would take to make the retreat to Northwest River. Finally I agreed that it was best to return. On the twenty-first of September the retreat was begun and Hubbard died on the eighteenth of October. Now, two years later, I realized that from Windbound Lake we could have reached Michikamau in five or six days at the very outside, and less than two weeks, allowing for delays through bad weather and our weakened condition, would have brought us to the George River, where, at that time of the year, ducks and ptarmigans are always plentiful. All these things I pondered as I sat by this camp fire, and I asked myself, "Why is it that when Fate closes our eyes she does not lead us aright?" Of course it is all conjecture, but I feel assured that if Hubbard and I had gone on then instead of turning back, Hubbard would still be with us.

Below the expansion on which our first camp on the river was pitched the stream trickled through the thickly strewn rocks in a wide bed, where it took a sharp turn to the northward and emptied into another expansion several miles in length, with probably a stream joining it from the northeast, though we were unable to investigate this, as high winds prevailed which made canoeing difficult, and we had to content ourselves with keeping a direct course.

It seemed as though with the crossing of the northern divide winter had come. On the night we reached the George River the temperature fell to ten degrees below the freezing point, and the following day it never rose above thirty-five degrees, and a high wind and snow squalls prevailed that held traveling in check. On the morning of the fifteenth we started forward in the teeth of a gale and the snow so thick we could not see the shore a storm that would be termed a "blizzard" in New York--and after two hours' hard work were forced to make a landing upon a sandy point with only a mile and a quarter to our credit.

Here we found the first real butchering camp of the Indians-- a camp of the previous spring. Piles of caribou bones that had been cracked to extract the marrow, many pairs of antlers, the bare poles of large lodges and extensive arrangements, such as racks and cross poles for dressing and curing deerskins. In a cache we found two muzzle-loading guns, cooking utensils, steel traps, and other camping and hunting paraphernalia.

On the portage around the last shallow rapid was a winter camp, where among other things was a komatik (dog sledge), showing that some of these Indians at least on the northern barrens used dogs for winter traveling. In the south of Labrador this would be quite out of the question, as there the bush is so thick that it does not permit the snow to drift and harden sufficiently to bear dogs, and the use of the komatik is therefore necessarily confined to the coast or near it. The Indian women there are very timid of the "husky" dogs, and the animals are not permitted near their camps.

The sixteenth of September--the day we passed through this large expansion--was Richards' birthday. When we bade good-by to the other men it was agreed that both parties should celebrate the day, wherever they might be, with the best dinner that could be provided from our respective stores. The meal was to be served at exactly seven o'clock in the evening, that we might feel on this one occasion that we were all sitting down to eat together, and fancy ourselves reunited. In the morning we opened the package that Richards gave us, and found in it a piece of fat pork and a quart of flour, intended for a feast of our favorite "darn goods." With self-sacrificing generosity he had taken these from the scanty rations they had allowed themselves for their return that we might have a pleasant surprise. With the now plentiful game this made it possible to prepare what seemed to us a very elaborate menu for the wild wastes of interior Labrador. First, there was bouillon, made from beef capsules; then an entrée of fried ptarmigan and duck giblets; a roast of savory black duck, with spinach (the last of our desiccated vegetables); and for dessert French toast 'a la Labrador (alias darn goods), followed by black coffee. When it was finished we spent the evening by the camp fire, smoking and talking of the three men retreating down our old trail, and trying to calculate at which one of the camping places they were bivouacked. Every night since our parting this had been our chief diversion, and I must confess that with each day that took us farther away from them an increased loneliness impressed itself upon us. Solemn and vast was the great silence of the trackless wilderness as more and more we came to realize our utter isolation from all the rest of the world and all mankind.

The marsh and swamp land gradually gave way to hills, which increased in size and ruggedness as we proceeded. We had found the river at its very beginning, and for a short way portages, as has been suggested, had to be made around shallow places, but after a little, as other streams augmented the volume of water, this became unnecessary, and as the river grew in size it became a succession of rapids, and most of them unpleasant ones, that kept us dodging rocks all the while.

Mr. A. P. Low, of the Canadian Geological Survey, in other parts of the Labrador interior found black ducks very scarce. This was not our experience. From the day we entered the George River until we were well down the stream they were plentiful, and we shot what we needed without turning our canoe out of its course to hunt them. This is apparently a breeding ground for them.

Several otter rubs were noted, and we saw some of the

animals, but did not disturb them. In places where the river broadened out and the current was slack every rock that stuck above the water held its muskrat house, and large numbers of the rats were seen.

After the snow we had one or two fine, bright days, but they were becoming few now, and the frosty winds and leaden skies, the forerunners of winter, were growing more and more frequent. When the bright days did come they were exceptional ones. I find noted in my diary one morning: "This is a morning for the gods--a morning that could scarcely be had anywhere in the world but in Labrador--a cloudless sky, no breath of wind, the sun rising to light the heavy hoarfrost and make it glint and sparkle till every tree and bush and rock seems made of shimmering silver."

One afternoon as we were passing through an expansion and I was scanning, as was my custom, every bit of shore in the hope of discovering a wigwam smoke, I saw, running down the side of a hill on an island a quarter of a mile away, a string of Indians waving wildly at us and signaling us to come ashore. After twelve weeks, in which not a human being aside from our own party had been seen, we had reached the dwellers of the wilderness, and with what pleasure and alacrity we accepted the invitation to join them can be imagined.

Chapter 13: Disaster in the Rapids

It was a hunting party--four men and a half-grown boy--with two canoes and armed with rifles. The Indians gave us the hearty welcome of the wilderness and received us like old friends. First, the chief, whose name was Toma, shook our hand, then the others, laughing and all talking at once in their musical Indian tongue. It was a welcome that said: "You are our brothers. You have come far to see us, and we are glad to have you with us."

After the first greetings were over they asked for stemmo, and I gave them each a plug of tobacco, for that is what stemmo means. They had no pipes with them, so I let them have two of mine, and it did my heart good to see the look of supreme satisfaction that crept into each dusky face as its possessor inhaled in long, deep pulls the smoke of the strong tobacco. It was like the food that comes to a half-starved man. After they had had their smoke, passing the pipes from mouth to mouth, I brought forth our kettle. In a jiffy they had a fire, and I made tea for them, which they drank so scalding hot it must have burned their throats. They told us they had had neither tea nor tobacco for a long while, and were very hungry for both. These are the stimulants of the Labrador Indians, and they will make great sacrifices to secure them.

All the time that this was taking place we were jabbering, each in his own tongue, neither we nor they understanding much that the other said. I did make out from them that we were the first white men that had ever visited them in their hunting grounds and that they were glad to see us.

Accepting an invitation to visit their lodges and escorted by a canoe on either side of ours, we finally turned down stream and, three miles below, came to the main camp of the Indians, which was situated, as most of their hunting camps are, on a slight eminence that commanded a view of the river for several miles in either direction, that watch might be constantly kept for bands of caribou.

We were discovered long before we arrived at the lodges, and were met by the whole population--men, women, children, dogs, and all. Our reception was tumultuous and cordial. It was a picturesque group. The swarthy-faced men, lean, sinewy and well built, with their long, straight black hair reaching to their shoulders, most of them hatless and all wearing a red bandanna handkerchief banded across the forehead, moccasined feet and multi-colored leggings; the women quaint and odd; the eager-faced children; little hunting dogs, and big wolf- like huskies.

All hands turned to and helped us carry our belongings to the camp, pitch our tent and get firewood for our stove. Then the men squatted around until eleven of them were with us in our little seven by nine tent, while all the others crowded as near to the entrance as they could. I treated everybody to hot tea. The men helped themselves first, then passed their cups on to the women and children. The used tea leaves from the kettle were carefully preserved by them to do service again. The eagerness with which the men and women drank the tea and smoked the tobacco aroused my sympathies, and I distributed amongst them all of these that I could well spare from our store. In appreciation of my gifts they brought us a considerable quantity of fresh and jerked venison and smoked fat; and Toma, as a special mark of favor presented me with a deer's tongue which had been cured by some distinctive process unlike anything I had ever eaten before, and it was delicious indeed, together with a bladder of refined fat so clear that it was almost transparent.

The encampment consisted of two deerskin wigwams. One was a large one and oblong in shape, the other of good size but round. The smaller wigwam was heated by a single fire in the center, the larger one by three fires distributed at intervals down its length. Chief Toma occupied, with his family, the smaller lodge, while the others made their home in the larger

97

one.

This was a band of Mountaineer Indians who trade at Davis Inlet Post of the Hudson's Bay Company, on the east coast, visiting the Post once or twice a year to exchange their furs for such necessaries as ammunition, clothing, tobacco and tea. Unlike their brothers on the southern slope, they have not accustomed themselves to the use of flour, sugar and others of the simplest luxuries of civilization, and their food is almost wholly flesh, fish and berries. They live in the crude, primordial fashion of their forefathers. To aid them in their hunt they have adopted the breech-loading rifle and muzzle-loading shotgun, but the bow and arrow has still its place with them and they were depending wholly upon this crude weapon for hunting partridges and other small game now, as they had no shotgun ammunition. The boys were constantly practicing with it while at play and were very expert in its use.

These Indians are of medium height, well built, sinewy and strong, alert and quick of movement. The women are generally squatty and fat, and the greater a woman's avoirdupois the more beautiful is she considered.

All the Mountaineer Indians of Labrador are nominally Roman Catholics. Those in the south are quite devoted to their priest, and make an effort to meet him at least once a year and pay their tithes, but here in the north this is not the case. In fact some of these people had seen their priest but once in their life and some of the younger ones had never seen him at all. Therefore they are still living under the influence of the ancient superstitions of their race, though the women are all provided with crucifixes and wear them on their breasts as ornaments.

They are perfectly honest. Indians, until they become contaminated by contact with whites, always are honest. It is the white man that teaches them to steal, either by actually pilfering from the ignorant savage, or by taking undue advantage of him in trade. Human nature is the same everywhere, and the Indian will, when he finds he is being taken advantage of and robbed, naturally resent it and try to "get even." Our things were left wholly unguarded, and were the object of a great deal of curiosity and admiration, not only our guns and instruments, but nearly everything we had, and were handled and inspected by our hosts, but not the slightest thing was filched. No Labrador Indian north of the Grand River will ever disturb a cache unless driven to it by the direst necessity, and even then will leave something in payment for what he takes.

We told them of the evidences we had seen of the caribou migration having taken place between Michikamau and Michikamats, and they were mightily interested. They had missed it but were, nevertheless, meeting small bands of caribou and making a good killing, as the quantities of meat hanging everywhere to dry for winter use bore evidence. The previous winter, they told us, was a hard one with them. Reindeer and ptarmigan disappeared, and before spring they were on the verge of starvation.

Our visit was made the occasion of a holiday and they devoted themselves wholly to our entertainment, and I believe were genuinely sorry when, on the afternoon after our arrival, I announced my decision to break camp and proceed. They helped us get ready, drew a rough sketch of the river so far as they knew it, and warned us to look out for numerous rapids and some high falls around which there was a portage trail. Farther on, they said, the river was joined by another, and then it became a "big, big river," and for two days' journey was good. Beyond that it was reported to be very bad. They had never traveled it, because they heard it was so bad, and they could not tell us, from their own knowledge, what it was like, but repeated the warning, "Shepoo matchi, shepoo matchi" (River bad), and told us to look out.

When we were ready to go, as a particular mark of good feeling, they brought us parting gifts of smoked deer's fat and were manifestly in earnest in their urgent invitations to us to come again. The whole encampment assembled at the shore to see us off and, as our canoes pushed out into the stream, the men pitched small stones after us as a good luck omen. If the stones hit you good luck is assured. You will have a good hunt and no harm will come to you. None of the stones happened to hit us. We could see the group waving at us until we rounded the point of land upon which the lodges stood; then the men all appeared on the other side of the point, where they had run to watch us until we disappeared around a bend in the river below, as we passed on to push our way deeper and deeper into the land of silence and mystery.

The following morning brought us into a lake expansion some twelve miles long and two miles or so in width, with a great many bays and arms which were extremely confusing to us in our search for the place where the river left it. The lower end was blocked with islands, and innumerable rocky bars, partially submerged, extended far out into the water. A strong southwest wind sent heavy rollers down the lake. Low, barren hills skirted the shores.

Early in the afternoon we turned into a bay where I left Easton with the canoe while I climbed one of the barren knolls. I had scarcely reached the summit when I heard a rifle shot, and then, after a pause, three more in quick succession. There were four cartridges in my rifle. I ran down to the canoe where I found Easton in wild excitement, waving the gun and calling for cartridges, and half-way across the bay saw the heads of two caribou swimming toward the opposite shore. I loaded the magazine and sat down to wait for the animals to land.

When the first deer got his footing and showed his body above the water three hundred and fifty yards away, I took him behind the shoulder. He dropped where he stood. The other animal stopped to look at his comrade, and a single bullet, also behind his shoulder, brought him down within ten feet of where he had stood when he was hit. I mention this to show the high efficiency of the .33 Winchester. At a comparatively long range two bullets had killed two caribou on the spot without the necessity of a chase after wounded animals, and one bullet had passed from behind the shoulder, the length of the neck, into the head and glancing downward had broken the jaw.

I desired to make a cache here that we might have something to fall back upon in case our retreat should become necessary, and four days were employed in fixing up the meat and preparing the cache, and this gave us also sufficient time, in spite of continuous heavy wind and rain, to thoroughly explore the lake and its bays. An ample supply of the fresh venison was reserved to carry with us.

We now had on hand, exclusive of the pemmican and other rations still remaining, and the meat cached, eight weeks' provisions, with plenty of ducks and ptarmigans everywhere, and there seemed to be no further danger from lack of food.

One day, while we were here, five caribou tarried for several minutes within two hundred yards of us and then sauntered off without taking alarm, and later the same day another was seen at closer range; but we did not need them and permitted them to go unmolested.

From a hill near this bay, where we killed the deer, on the eastern side of the lake, we discovered a trail leading off toward a string of lakes to the eastward. This is undoubtedly the portage trail which the Indians follow in their journeys to the Post at Davis Inlet. Toma had told me we might see it here, and that, not far in, on one of these lakes was another Indian camp.

An inordinate craving for fat takes possession of every one after a little while in the bush. We had felt it, and now, with plenty, overindulged, with the result that we were attacked with illness, and for a day or two I was almost too sick to move.

The morning we left Atuknipi, or Reindeer Lake, as we shall call the expansion, a blinding snowstorm was raging, with a strong head wind. Several rapids were run though it was extremely dangerous work, for at times we could scarcely see a dozen yards ahead. At midday the snow ceased, but the wind increased in velocity until finally we found it quite out of the question to paddle against it, and were forced to pitch camp on the shores of a small expansion and under the lee of a hill. For two days the gale blew unceasingly and held us prisoners in our camp. The waves broke on the rocky shores, sending the spray fifty feet in the air and, freezing on the surrounding boulders, covered them with a glaze of ice. I cannot say what the temperature was, for on the day of our arrival here my last thermometer was broken; but with half a foot of snow on the ground, the freezing spray and the bitter cold wind, we were warned that winter was reaching out her hand toward Labrador and would soon hold us in her merciless grasp. This made me chafe under our imprisonment, for I began to fear that we should not reach the Post before the final freeze-up came, and further travel by canoe would be out of the question. On the morning of September twenty-ninth, the wind, though still blowing half a gale in our faces, had so much abated that we were able to launch our canoe and continue our journey.

It was very cold. The spray froze as it struck our clothing, the, canoe was weighted with ice and our paddles became heavy with it. We ran one or two short rapids in safety and then started into another that ended with a narrow strip of white water with a small expansion below. We had just struck the white water, going at a good speed in what seemed like a clear course, when the canoe, at its middle, hit a submerged rock. Before there was time to clear ourselves the little craft swung in the current, and the next moment I found myself in the rushing, seething flood rolling down through the rocks.

When I came to the surface I was in the calm water below the rapid and twenty feet away was the canoe, bottom up, with Easton clinging to it, his clothing fast on a bolt under the canoe. I swam to him and, while he drew his hunting knife and cut himself loose, steadied the canoe. We had neglected--and it was gross carelessness in us--to tie our things fast, and the lighter bags and paddles were floating away while everything that was heavy had sunk beyond hope of recovery. The thwarts, however, held fast in the overturned canoe a bag of pemmican, one other small bag, the tent and tent stove. Treading water to keep ourselves afloat we tried to right the canoe to save these, but our efforts were fruitless. The icy water so benumbed us we could scarcely control our limbs. The tracking line was fast to the stern thwart, and with one end of this in his teeth, Easton swam to a little rocky island just below the rapid and hauled while I swam by the canoe and steadied the things under the thwarts. It took us half an hour to get the canoe ashore, and we could hardly stand when he had it righted and the water emptied out.

Then I looked for wood to build a fire, for I knew that unless we could get artificial heat immediately we would perish with the cold, for the very blood in our veins was freezing. Not a stick was there nearer than an eighth of a mile across the bay. Our paddles were gone, but we got into the canoe and used our hands for paddles. By the time we landed Easton had grown very pale. He began picking and clutching aimlessly at the trees. The blood had congealed in my hands until they were so stiff as to be almost useless. I could not guide them to the trousers pocket at first where I kept my waterproof match- box. Finally I loosened my belt and found the matches, and with the greatest difficulty managed to get one between my benumbed fingers, and scratched it on the bottom of the box. The box was wet and the match head flew off. Everything was wet. Not a dry stone even stuck above the snow. I tried another match on the box, but, like the first, the head flew off, and then another and another with the same result. Under ordinary circumstances I could have secured a light somehow and quickly, but now my hands and fingers were stiff as sticks and refused to grip the matches firmly. I worked with desperation, but it seemed hopeless. Easton's face by this time had taken on the waxen shade that comes with death, and he appeared to be looking through a haze. His senses were leaving him. I saw something must be done at once, and I shouted to him: "Run! run! Easton, run!" Articulation was difficult, and I did not know my own voice. It seemed very strange and far away to me. We tried to run but had lost control of our legs and both fell down. With an effort I regained my feet but fell again when I tried to go forward. My legs refused to carry me. I crawled on my hands and knees in the snow for a short distance, and it was all I could do to recover my feet. Easton had now lost all understanding of his surroundings. He was looking into space but saw nothing. He was groping blindly with his hands. He did not even know that he was cold. I saw that only a fire could save his life, and perhaps mine, and that we must have it quickly, and made one more superhuman effort with the matches. One after another I tried them with the same result as before until but three remained. All depended upon those three matches. The first one flickered for a moment and my hopes rose, but my poor benumbed fingers refused to hold it and it fell into the snow and went out. The wind was drying the box bottom. I tried another--an old sulphur match, I remember. It burned! I applied it with the greatest care to a handful of the hairy moss that is found under the branches next the trunk of spruce trees, and this ignited. Then I put on small sticks, nursing the blaze with the greatest care, adding larger sticks as the smaller ones took fire. I had dropped on my knees and could reach the sticks from where I knelt, for there was plenty of dead wood lying about. As the blaze grew I rose to my feet and, dragging larger wood, piled it on. A sort of joyful mania took possession of me as I watched the great tongues of flames shooting skyward and listened to the crackling of the burning wood, and I stood back and laughed. I had triumphed over fate and the elements. Our arms, our clothing, nearly all our food, our axes and our paddles, and even the means of making new paddles were gone, but for the present we were safe. Life, no matter how uncertain, is sweet, and I laughed with the very joy of living.

Chapter 14: Tide Water and the Post

When Easton came to his senses, he found himself warming by the fire. It is wonderful how quickly a half-frozen man will revive. As soon as we were thoroughly thawed out we stripped to our underclothing and hung our things up to dry, permitting our underclothing to dry on us as we stood near the blaze. We were little the worse for our dip, escaping with slightly frosted fingers and toes. I discovered in my pockets a half plug of black tobacco such as we use in the North, put it on the end of a stick and dried it out, and then we had a smoke. We agreed that we had never in our life before had so satisfactory a smoke as that. The stimulant was needed and it put new life into us.

Easton was very pessimistic. He was generally inclined to look upon the dark side of things anyway, and now he believed our fate was sealed, especially if we could not find our paddles, and he began to talk about returning to our cache and thence to the Indians. But I had been in much worse predicaments than this, and paddles or no paddles, determined to go on, for we could work our way down the river somehow with poles and the bag of pemmican would keep us alive until we reached the Post--unless the freeze-up caught us.

When we had dried ourselves we went to the canoe to make an inventory of our remaining goods and chattels, and with a vague hope that a paddle might be found on the shore. What, then, was our surprise and our joy to find not only the paddles but our dunnage bags and my instrument bag amongst the rocks, where an eddy below the rapid swirled the water in. Thus our blankets and clothing were safe, we had fifty pounds of pemmican, our tent and tent stove, and in the small bag that I have mentioned as having remained in the canoe with the other things was all our tea and five or six pounds of caribou tallow. Our matches--and this was a great piece of good fortune--were uninjured, and we had a good stock of them. The tent stove seemed useless without the pipe, but we determined to cling to it, as our luggage now was light. Our guns, axes, the balance of our provisions, including salt, the tea kettle and all our other cooking utensils, were gone, and worst of all, three hundred and fifty unexposed photographic films. Only twenty or thirty unexposed films were saved, but fortunately, only one roll of ten exposed films, which was in one of the cameras, was injured, and none of the exposed films was lost. One camera was damaged beyond use, as were also my aneroid barometer and binoculars. However, we were fortunate to get off so easily as we did, and the accident taught us the lesson to take no chances in rapids and to tie everything fast at all times. Carelessness is pretty sure to demand its penalty, and the wilderness is constantly springing surprises upon those who submit themselves to its care.

A pretty dreary camp we pitched that evening near the place of our mishap. Fortunately there was plenty of dead wood loose on the ground, and we did very well for our camp fire without the axes. A pemmican can with the end cut off about an inch from the top, with a piece of copper wire that I found in my dunnage bag fashioned into a bale, made a very serviceable tea pail, from which we drank in turn, as our cups were lost. The top of the can answered for a frying pan in which to melt our caribou tallow and pemmican when we wanted our ration hot, and as a plate. Tent pegs were cut with our jackknives and the tent stretched between two trees, which avoided the necessity of tent poles. Thus, with our cooking and living outfit reduced to the simplest and crudest form, and with a limited and unvaried diet of pemmican, tallow and tea, we were on the whole able, so long as loose wood could be found for our night camps, to keep comparatively comfortable and free from any severe hardships.

We certainly had great reason to be thankful, and that night before we rolled into our blankets I read aloud by the light of our camp fire from my little Bible the one hundred and seventh Psalm, in thanksgiving.

The next morning before starting forward we paddled out to

the rapid, in the vain hope that we might be able to recover some of the lost articles from the bottom of the river, but at the place where the spill had occurred the water was too swift and deep for us to do anything, and we were forced to abandon the attempt and reluctantly resume our journey without the things.

That night we felt sorely the loss of the axes. Our camp was pitched in a spot where no loose wood was to be found save very small sticks, insufficient in quantity for an adequate fire in the open, for the evening was cold. We could not pitch our tent wigwam fashion with an opening at the top for the smoke to escape, as to do that several poles were necessary, and we had no means of cutting them. However, with the expectation that enough smoke would find its way out of the stovepipe hole to permit us to remain inside, we built a small round Indian fire in the center of the tent. We managed to endure the smoke and warm ourselves while tea was making, but the experiment proved a failure and was not to be resorted to again, for I feared it might result in an attack of smoke-blindness. This is an affliction almost identical in effect to snow-blindness. I had suffered from it in the first days of my wandering alone in the Susan Valley in the winter of 1903, and knew what it meant, and that an attack of it would preclude traveling while it lasted, to say nothing of the pain that it would inflict.

Here a portage was necessary around a half-mile canyon through which the river, a rushing torrent, tumbled in the interval over a series of small falls, and all the way the perpendicular walls of basaltic rock that confined it rose on either side to a height of fifty to seventy- five feet above the seething water. Just below this canyon another river joined us from the east, increasing the volume of water very materially. Our tumplines were gone, but with the tracking line and pieces of deer skin we improvised new ones that answered our purpose very well.

The hills, barren almost to their base, and growing in altitude with every mile we traveled, were now closely hugging the river valley, which was almost destitute of trees. Rapids were practically continuous and always strewn with dangerous rocks that kept us constantly on the alert and our nerves strung to the highest tension.

The general course of the river for several days was north,

thirty degrees east, but later assumed an almost due northerly course. It made some wide sweeps as it worked its tortuous way through the ranges, sometimes almost doubling on itself. At intervals small streams joined it and it was constantly growing in width and depth. Once we came to a place where it dropped over massive bed rock in a series of falls, some of which were thirty or more feet in height. Few portages, however, were necessary. We took our chances on everything that there was any prospect of the canoe living through-- rapids that under ordinary circumstances we should never have trusted --for the grip of the cold weather was tightening with each October day. The small lakes away from the river, where the water was still, must even now have been frozen, but the river current was so big and strong that it had as yet warded off the frost shackles. When the real winter came, however, it would be upon us in a night, and then even this mighty torrent must submit to its power.

At one point the valley suddenly widened and the hills receded, and here the river broke up into many small streams-- no less than five-- but some four or five miles farther on these various channels came together again, and then the growing hills closed in until they pinched the river banks more closely than ever.

On the morning of October sixth we swung around a big bend in the river, ran a short but precipitous rapid and suddenly came upon another large river flowing in from the west. This stream came through a sandy valley, and below the junction of the rivers the sand banks rose on the east side a hundred feet or so above the water. The increase here in the size of the stream was marked--it was wide and deep. A terrific gale was blowing and caught us directly in our faces as we turned the bend and lost the cover of the lee share above the curve, and paddling ahead was impossible. The waves were so strong, in fact, that we barely escaped swamping before we effected a landing.

We here found ourselves in an exceedingly unpleasant position. We were only fitted with summer clothing, which was now insufficient protection. There was not enough loose wood to make an open fire to keep us warm for more than an hour or so, and we could not go on to look for a better camping place. In a notch between the sand ridges we found a small cluster of trees, between two of which our tent was stretched, but it was mighty uncomfortable with no means of warming. "If we only had our stovepipe now we'd be able to break enough small stuff to keep the stove going," said Easton. With nothing else to do we climbed a knoll to look at the river below, and there on the knoll what should we find but several lengths of nearly worn-out but still serviceable pipe that some Indian had abandoned. "It's like Robinson Crusoe," said Easton. "Just as soon as we need something that we can't get on very well without we find it. A special Providence is surely caring for us." We appropriated that pipe, all right, and it did not take us long to get a fire in the stove, which we had clung to, useless as it had seemed to be.

A mass of ripe cranberries, so thick that we crushed them with every step, grew on the hills, and we picked our pailful and stewed them, using crystallose (a small phial of which I had in my dunnage bag) as sweetening. A pound of pemmican a day with a bit of tallow is sustaining, but not filling, and left us with a constant, gnawing hunger. These berries were a godsend, and sour as they were we filled up on them and for once gratified our appetites. We had a great desire, too, for something sweet, and always pounced upon the stray raisins in the pemmican. When either of us found one in his ration it was divided between us. Our great longing was for bread and molasses, just as it had been with Hubbard and me when we were short of food, and we were constantly talking of the feasts we would have of these delicacies when we reached the Post--wheat bread and common black molasses.

The George River all the way down to this point had been in past years a veritable slaughter house. There were great piles of caribou antlers (the barren-ground caribou or reindeer), sometimes as many as two or three hundred pairs in a single pile, where the Indians had speared the animals in the river, and everywhere along the banks were scattered dry bones. Abandoned camps, and some of them large ones and not very old, were distributed at frequent intervals, though we saw no more of the Indians themselves until we reached Ungava Bay.

Wolves were numerous. We saw their tracks in the sand and fresh signs of them were common. They always abound where there are caribou, which form their main living. Ptarmigans in the early morning clucked on the river banks like chickens in a barnyard, and we saw some very large flocks of them. Geese and black ducks, making their way to the southward, were met with daily. But we had no arms or ammunition with which to kill them. I saw some fox signs, but there were very few or no rabbit signs, strange to say, until we were a full hundred miles farther down the river.

This camp, where we found the stovepipe, we soon discovered was nearly at the head of Indian House Lake, so called by a Hudson's Bay Company factor-John McLean-because of the numbers of Indians that he found living on its shores. McLean, about seventy years earlier, had ascended the river in the interests of his company, for the purpose of establishing interior posts. The most inland Post that he erected was at the lower end of this lake, which is fifty-five miles in length. He also built a Post on a large lake which he describes in his published journal as lying to the west of Indian House Lake. The exact location of this latter lake is not now known, but I am inclined to think it is one which the Indians say is the source of Whale River, a stream of considerable size emptying into Ungava Bay one hundred and twenty miles to the westward of the mouth of the George River. These two rivers are doubtless much nearer together, however, farther inland, where Whale River has its rise. The difficulty experienced by McLean in getting supplies to these two Posts rendered them unprofitable, and after experimenting with them for three years they were abandoned. The agents in charge were each spring on the verge of starvation before the opening of the waters brought fish and food or they were relieved by the brigades from Ungava. They had to depend almost wholly upon their hunters for provisions. It was not attempted in those days to carry in flour, pork and other food stuffs now considered by the traders necessaries. And almost the only goods handled by them in the Indian trade were axes, knives, guns, ammunition and beads.

Indian House Lake now, as then, is a general rendezvous for the Indians during the summer months, when they congregate there to fish and to hunt reindeer. In the autumn they scatter to the better trapping grounds, where fur bearing animals are found in greater abundance. We were too late in the season to meet these Indians, though we saw many of their camping places.

A snowstorm began on October seventh, but the wind had so far abated that we were able to resume our journey. It was a bleak and dismal day. Save for now and then a small grove of spruce trees in some sheltered nook, and these at long intervals, the country was destitute and barren of growth. Below our camp, upon entering the lake, there was a wide, flat stretch of sand wash from the river, and below this from the lake shore on either side, great barren, grim hills rose in solemn majesty, across whose rocky face the wind swept the snow in fitful gusts and squalls. Off on a mountain side a wolf disturbed the white silence with his dismal cry, and farther on a big black fellow came to the water's edge, and with the snow blowing wildly about him held his head in the air and howled a challenge at us as we passed close by. Perhaps he yearned for companionship and welcomed the sight of living things. For my part, grim and uncanny as be looked, I was glad to see him. He was something to vary the monotony of the great solemn silence of our world.

The storm increased, and early in the day the snow began to fall so heavily that we could not see our way, and forced us to turn into a bay where we found a small cluster of trees amongst big boulders, and pitched our tent in their shelter. The snow had drifted in and filled the space between the rocks, and on this we piled armfuls of scraggy boughs and made a fairly level and wholly comfortable bed; but it was a long, tedious job digging with our hands and feet into the snow for bits of wood for our stove. The conditions were growing harder and harder with every day, and our experience here was a common one with us for the most of the remainder of the way down the river from this point.

The day we reached the lower end of the lake I summed up briefly its characteristics in my field book as follows:

"Indian House Lake has a varying width of from a quarter mile to three miles. It is apparently not deep. Both shores are followed by ridges of the most barren, rocky hills imaginable, some of them rising to a height of eight to nine hundred feet and sloping down sharply to the shores, which are strewn with large loose boulders or are precipitous bed rock. An occasional sand knoll occurs, and upon nearly every one of these is an abandoned Indian camp. The timber growth--none at all or very scanty spruce and tamarack. Length of lake (approximated) fifty-five miles."

I had hoped to locate the site of McLean's old Post buildings, more than three score years ago destroyed by the Indians, doubtless for firewood, but the snow had bidden what few traces of them time had not destroyed, and they were passed unnoticed. The storm which raged all the time we were here made progress slow, and it was not until the morning of the tenth that we reached the end of the lake, where the river, vastly increased in volume, poured out through a rapid.

Below Indian House Lake there were only a few short stretches of slack water to relieve the pretty continuous rapids. The river wound in and out, in and out, rushing on its tumultuous way amongst ever higher mountains. There was no time to examine the rapids before we shot them. We had to take our chances, and as we swung around every curve we half expected to find before us a cataract that would hurl us to destruction. The banks were often sheer from the water's edge, and made landing difficult or even impossible. In one place for a distance of many miles the river had worn its way through the mountains, leaving high, perpendicular walls of solid rock on either side, forming a sort of canyon. In other places high boulders, piled by some giant force, formed fifty-foot high walls, which we had to scale each night to make our camp. In the morning some peak in the blue distance would be noted as a landmark. In a couple of hours we would rush past it and mark another one, which, too, would soon be left behind.

The rapids continued the characteristic of the river and were terrific. Often it would seem that no canoe could ride the high, white waves, or that we could not avoid the swirl of mighty cross- current eddies, which would have swallowed up our canoe like a chip had we got into them. There were rapids whose roar could be distinctly heard for five or six miles. These we approached with the greatest care, and portaged around the worst places. The water was so clear that often we found ourselves dodging rocks, which, when we passed them, were ten or twelve feet below the surface. It was here that a peculiar optical illusion occurred. The water appeared to be running down an incline of about twenty degrees. At the place where this was noticed, however, the current was not exceptionally swift. We were in a section now where the Indians never go, owing to the character of the river--a section that is wholly untraveled and unhunted.

After leaving Indian House Lake, as we descended from the plateau, the weather grew milder. There were chilly winds and bleak rains, but the snow, though remaining on the mountains, disappeared gradually from the valley, and this was a blessing to us, for it enabled us to make camp with a little less labor, and the bits of wood were left uncovered, to be gathered with more ease. Every hour of light we needed, for with each dawn and twilight the days were becoming noticeably shorter. The sun now rose in the southeast, crossed a small segment of the sky, and almost before we were aware of it set in the southwest.

The wilderness gripped us closer and closer as the days went by. Remembrances of the outside world were becoming like dreamland fancies--something hazy, indefinite and unreal. We could hardly bring ourselves to believe that we had really met the Indians. It seemed to us that all our lives we had been going on and on through rushing water, or with packs over rocky portages, and the Post we were aiming to reach appeared no nearer to us than it did the day we left Northwest River--long, long ago. We seldom spoke. Sometimes in a whole day not a dozen words would be exchanged. If we did talk at all it was at night over soothing pipes, after the bit of pemmican we allowed ourselves was disposed of, and was usually of something to eat--planning feasts of darn goods, bread and molasses when we should reach a place where these luxuries were to be had. It was much like the way children plan what wonderful things they will do, and what unbounded good things they will indulge in, when they attain that high pinnacle of their ambition-- "grown-ups."

After our upset in the rapid Easton eschewed water entirely, except for drinking purposes. He had had enough of it, he said. I did bathe my hands and face occasionally, particularly in the morning, to rouse me from the torpor of the always heavy sleep of night. What savages men will revert into when they are buried for a long period in the wilderness and shake off the trammels and customs of the conventionalism of civilization! It does not take long to make an Indian out of a white man so far as habits and customs of living go.

Our routine of daily life was always the same. Long before daylight I would arise, kindle a fire, put over it our tea water, and then get Easton out of his blankets. At daylight we would start. At midday we had tea, and at twilight made the best camp we could.

The hills were assuming a different aspect--less conical in form and not so high. The boulders on the river banks were superseded by massive bed-rock granite. The coves and hollows were better wooded and there were some stretches of slack water. On October fifteenth we portaged around a series of low falls, below which was a small lake expansion with a river flowing into it from the east. Here we found the first evidence of human life that we had seen in a long while--a wide portage trail that had been cut through now burned and dead trees on the eastern side of the river. It was fully six feet in width and had been used for the passage of larger boats than canoes. The moss was still unrenewed where the tramp of many moccasins had worn it off. This was the trail made by John McLean's brigades nearly three-quarters of a century before, for in their journeys to Indian House Lake they had used rowboats and not canoes for the transportation of supplies.

The day we passed over this portage was a most miserable one. We were soaked from morning till night with mingled snow and rain, and numb with the cold, but when we made our night camp, below the junction of the rivers, one or two ax cuttings were found, and I knew that now our troubles were nearly at an end and we were not far from men. The next afternoon (Monday, October sixteenth) we stopped two or three miles below a rapid to boil our kettle, and before our tea was made the canoe was high and dry on the rocks. We had reached tide water at last! How we hurried through that luncheon, and with what light hearts we launched the canoe again, and how we peered into every bay for the Post buildings that we knew were now close at hand can be imagined. These bays were being left wide stretches of mud and rocks by the receding water, which has a tide fall here of nearly forty feet. At last, as we rounded a rocky point, we saw the Post. The group of little white buildings nestling deep in a cove, a feathery curl of smoke rising peacefully from the agent's house, an Eskimo tupek (tent), boats standing high on the mud flat below, and the howl of a husky dog in the distance, formed a picture of comfort that I shall long remember.

Chapter 15: Off with the Eskimos

The tide had left the bay drained, on the farther side and well toward the bottom of which the Post stands, and between us and the buildings was a lake of soft mud. There seemed no approach for the canoe, and rather than sit idly until the incoming tide covered the mud again so that we could paddle in, we carried our belongings high up the side of the hill, safely out of reach of the water when it should rise, and then started to pick our way around the face of the clifflike hill, with the intention of skirting the bay and reaching the Post at once from the upper side.

It was much like walking on the side of a wall, and to add to our discomfiture night began to fall before we were half way around, for it was slow work. Once I descended cautiously to the mud, thinking that I might be able to walk across it, but a deep channel filled with running water intercepted me, and I had to return to Easton, who had remained above. We finally realized that we could not get around the hill before dark and the footing was too uncertain to attempt to retrace our steps to the canoe in the fading light, as a false move would have hurled us down a hundred feet into the mud and rocks below. Fortunately a niche in the hillside offered a safe resting place, and we drew together here all the brush within reach, to be burned later as a signal to the Post folk that someone was on the hill, hoping that when the tide rose it would bring them in, a boat to rescue us from our unpleasant position. When the brush was arranged for firing at an opportune time we sat down in the thickening darkness to watch the lights which were now flickering cozily in the windows of the Post house.

116

"Well, this is hard luck," said Easton. "There's good bread and molasses almost within hailing distance and we've likely got to sit out here on the rocks all night without wood enough to keep fire, and it's going to rain pretty soon and we can't even get back to our pemmican and tent."

"Don't give up yet, boy," I encouraged. "Maybe they'll see our fire when we start it and take us off."

We filled our pipes and struck matches to light them. They were wax taper matches and made a good blaze. "Wonder what it'll be like to eat civilized grub again and sleep in a bed," said Easton meditatively, as he puffed uncomfortably at his pipe.

While he was speaking the glow of a lantern appeared from the Post house, which we could locate by its lamp-lit windows, and moved down toward the place where we had seen the boats on the mud. The sight of it made us hope that we had been noticed, and we jumped up and combined our efforts in shouting until we were hoarse. Then we ignited the pile of brush. It blazed up splendidly, shooting its flames high in the air, sending its sparks far, and lighting weirdly the strange scene. We stood before it that our forms might appear in relief against the light reflected by the rocky background, waving our arms and renewing our shouts. Once or twice I fancied I heard an answering hail from the other side, like a far-off echo; but the wind was against us and I was not sure. The lantern light was now in a boat moving out toward the main river. Even though it were coming to us this was necessary, as the tide could not be high enough yet to permit its coming directly across to where we were. We watched its course anxiously. Finally it seemed to be heading toward us, but we were not certain. Then it disappeared altogether and there was nothing but blackness and silence where it had been.

"Someone that's been waiting for the tide to turn and he's just going down the river, where he likely lives," remarked Easton as we sat down again and relit our pipes. "I began to taste bread and molasses when I saw that light," he continued, after a few minutes' pause. "It's just our luck. We're in for a night of it, all right."

We sat smoking silently, resigned to our fate, when all at once there stepped out of the surrounding darkness into the radius of light cast by our now dying fire, an old Eskimo with

117

an unlighted lantern in his hands, and a young fellow of fifteen or sixteen years of age.

"Oksutingyae," * said the Eskimo, and then proceeded to light his lantern, paying no further attention to us. "How do you do?" said the boy.

* [Dual form meaning "You two be strong," used by the Eskimos as a greeting. The singular of the same is Oksunae, and the plural (more than two) Oksusi]

The Eskimo could understand no English, but the boy, a grandson of John Ford, the Post agent, told us that the Eskimo had seen us strike the matches to light our pipes and reported the matter at once at the house. There was not a match at the Post nor within a hundred miles of it, so far as they knew, so Mr. Ford concluded that some strangers were stranded on the hill--possibly Eskimos in distress--and he gave them a lantern and started them over in a boat to investigate. Their lantern had blown out on the way--that was when we missed the light.

With the lantern to guide us we descended the slippery rocks to their boat and in ten minutes landed on the mud flat opposite, where we were met by Ford and a group of curious Eskimos. We were immediately con- ducted to the agent's residence, where Mrs. Ford received us in the hospitable manner of the North, and in a little while spread before us a delicious supper of fresh trout, white bread such as we had not seen since leaving Tom Blake's, mossberry jam and tea. It was an event in our life to sit down again to a table covered with white linen and eat real bread. We ate until we were ashamed of ourselves, but not until we were satisfied (for we had emerged from the bush with unholy appetites) and barely stopped eating in time to save our reputations from utter ruin. And now our hosts told us--and it shows how really generous and open-hearted they were to say nothing about it until we were through eating--that the Pelican, the Hudson's Bay Company's steamer, had not arrived on her annual visit, that it was so late in the season all hope of her coming had some time since been relinquished, and the Post provisions were reduced to forty pounds of flour, a bit of sugar, a barrel or so of corn meal, some salt pork and salt beef, and small quantities of other food stuffs, and there were a great many dependents with hungry mouths to feed. Molasses, butter and other things were entirely

118

gone. The storehouses were empty.

This condition of affairs made it incumbent upon me, I believed, in spite of a cordial invitation from Ford to stay and share with them what they had, to move on at once and endeavor to reach Fort Chimo ahead of the ice. Fort Chimo is the chief establishment of the fur trading companies on Ungava Bay, and is the farthest off and most isolated station in northern Labrador. This journey would be too hazardous to undertake in the month of October in a canoe--the rough, open sea of Ungava Bay demanded a larger craft--and although Ford told me it was foolhardy to attempt it so late in the season with any craft at all, I requested him to do his utmost the following day to engage for us Eskimos and a small boat and we would make the attempt to get there. It has been my experience that frontier traders are wont to overestimate the dangers in trips of this kind, and I was inclined to the belief that this was the case with Ford. In due time I learned my mistake.

Ford had no tobacco but the soggy black chewing plug dispensed to Eskimos, and we shared with him our remaining plugs and for two hours sat in the cozy Post house kitchen smoking and chatting. Over a year had passed since his last communication with the outside world, for no vessel other than the Pelican when she makes her annual call with supplies ever comes here, and we therefore had some things of interest to tell him.

Our host I soon discovered to be a man of intelligence. He was sixty-six years of age, a native of the east coast of Labrador, with a tinge of Eskimo blood in his veins, and as familiar with the Eskimo language as with English. For twenty years, he informed me, with the exception of one or two brief intervals, he had been buried at George River Post, and was longing for the time when he could leave it and enjoy the comforts of civilization.

After our chat we were shown to our room, where the almost forgotten luxuries of feather beds and pillows, and the great, warm, fluffy woolen blankets of the Hudson's Bay Company-- such blankets as are found nowhere else in the world--awaited us. To undress and crawl between them and lie there, warm and snug and dry, while we listened to the rain, which had begun beating furiously against the window and on the roof, and the wind howling around the house, seemed to me at first the pinnacle of comfort; but this sense of luxury soon passed off and I found myself longing for the tent and spruce-bough couch on the ground, where there was more air to breathe and a greater freedom. I could not sleep. The bed was too warm and the four walls of the room seemed pressing in on me. After four months in the open it takes some time for one to accustom one's self to a bed again.

The next day at high tide, with the aid of a boat and two Eskimos, we recovered our things from the rocks where we had cached them.

There were no Eskimos at the Post competent or willing to attempt the open-boat journey to Fort Chimo. Those that were here all agreed that the ice would come before we could get through and that it was too dangerous an undertaking. Therefore, galling as the delay was to me, there was nothing for us to do but settle down and wait for the time to come when we could go with dog teams overland.

On Thursday afternoon, three days after our arrival at the Post, we saw the Eskimos running toward the wharf and shouting as though something of unusual importance were taking place and, upon joining the crowd, found them greeting three strange Eskimos who had just arrived in a boat. The real cause of the excitement we soon learned was the arrival of the Pelican. The strange Eskimos were the pilots that brought her from Fort Chimo. All was confusion and rejoicing at once. Ford manned a boat and invited us to join him in a visit to the ship, which lay at anchor four miles below, and we were soon off.

When we boarded the Pelican, which, by the way, is an old British cruiser, we were received by Mr. Peter McKenzie, from Montreal, who has superintendence of eastern posts, and Captain Lovegrow, who commanded the vessel. They told us that they had called at Rigolet on their way north and there heard of the arrival of Richards, Pete and Stanton at Northwest River. This relieved my mind as to their safety.

We spent a very pleasant hour over a cigar, and heard the happenings in the outside world since our departure from it, the most important of which was the close of the Russian-Japanese war. We also learned that the cause of delay in the ship's coming was an accident on the rocks near Cartwright, making it necessary for them to run to St. Johns for repairs; and also that only the fact of the distressful condition of the Post, unprovisioned as they knew it must be, had induced them to take the hazard of running in and chancing imprisonment for the winter in the ice.

Mr. McKenzie extended me a most cordial invitation to return with them to Rigolet, but the Eskimo pilots had brought news of large herds of reindeer that the Indians had reported as heading eastward toward the Koksoak, the river on which Fort Chimo is situated, and I determined to make an effort to see these deer. This determination was coupled with a desire to travel across the northern peninsula and around the coast in winter and learn more of the people and their life than could be observed at the Post; and I therefore declined Mr. McKenzie's invitation.

Captain James Blanford, from St. Johns, was on board, acting as ship's pilot for the east coast, and he kindly offered to carry out for me such letters and telegrams as I might desire to send and personally attend to their transmission. I gladly availed myself of this offer, as it gave us an opportunity to relieve the anxiety of our friends at home as to our safety. Captain Blanford had been with the auxiliary supply ship of the Peary Arctic expedition during the summer and told us of having left Commander Peary at eighty degrees north latitude in August. The expedition, he told us, would probably winter as high as eighty-three degrees north, and he was highly enthusiastic over the good prospects of Peary's success in at least reaching "Farthest North."

The Eskimo pilots of the Pelican were more venturesome than their friends at George River. They had a small boat belonging to the Hudson's Bay Company, and in it were going to attempt to reach Fort Chimo. Against his advice I had Ford arrange with them to permit Easton and me to accompany them. It was a most fortunate circumstance, I thought, that this opportunity was opened to us.

Accordingly the letters for Captain Blanford were written, sufficient provisions, consisting of corn meal, flour, hard-tack, pork, and tea to last Easton and me ten days, were packed, and our luggage was taken on board the Pelican on Saturday afternoon, where we were to spend the night as Mr. McKenzie's

121

and Captain Lovegrow's guests.

Mr. McKenzie, before going to Montreal, had lived nearly a quarter of a century as Factor at Fort Chimo, and, thoroughly familiar with the conditions of the country and the season, joined Ford in advising us strongly against our undertaking, owing to the unusual hazard attached to it, and the probability of getting caught in the ice and wrecked. But we were used to hardship, and believed that if the Eskimos were willing to attempt the journey we could get through with them some way, and I saw no reason why I should change my plans.

Low-hanging clouds, flying snowflakes and a rising northeast wind threatened a heavy storm on Sunday morning, October twenty-second, when the Pelican weighed anchor at ten o'clock, with us on board and the small boat, the Explorer, that was to carry us westward in tow, and steamed down the George River, at whose mouth, twenty miles below, we were to leave her, to meet new and unexpected dangers and hardships.

At the Post the river is a mile and a half in width. About eight miles farther down its banks close in and "the Narrows" occur, and then it widens again. There is very little growth of any kind below the Narrows. The rocks are polished smooth and bare as they rise from the water's edge, and it is as desolate and barren a land as one's imagination could picture, but withal possesses a rugged grand beauty in its grim austerity that is impressive.

About three or four miles above the open bay the Pelican's engines ceased to throb and the Explorer was hauled alongside. Everything but the provisions for the Eskimo crew was already aboard. We said a hurried adieu and, watching our chances as the boat rose and fell on the swell, dropped one by one into the little craft. A bag of ship's biscuit, the provisions of our Eskimos, was thrown after us. Most of them went into the sea and were lost, and we needed them sadly later. I thought we should swamp as each sea hit us before we could get away, and when we were finally off the boat was half full of water.

The Eskimos hoisted a sail and turned to the west bank of the river, for it was too rough outside to risk ourselves there in the little Explorer. The pulse of the big ship began to beat and slowly she steamed out into the open and left us to the mercies of the unfeeling rocks of Ungava.

Chapter 16: Caught by the Arctic Ice

We ran to shelter in a small cove and under the lee of a ledge pitched our tent, using poles that the Eskimos had thoughtfully provided, and anchoring the tent down with boulders.

When I say the rocks here are scoured bare, I mean it literally. There was not a stick of wood growing as big as your finger. On the lower George, below the Narrows, and for long distances on the Ungava coast there is absolutely not a tree of any kind to be seen. The only exception is in one or two bays or near the mouth of streams, where a stunted spruce growth is sometimes found in small patches. There are places where you may skirt the coast of Ungava Bay for a hundred miles and not see a shrub worthy the name of tree, even in the bays.

The Koksoak (Big) River, on which Fort Chimo is situated, is the largest river flowing into Ungava Bay. The George is the second in size, and Whale River ranks third. Between the George River and Whale River there are four smaller ones-- Tunulik (Back) River, Kuglotook (Overflow) River, Tuktotuk (Reindeer) River and Mukalik (Muddy) River; and between Whale River and the Koksoak the False River. I crossed all of these streams and saw some of them for several miles above the mouth. The Koksoak, Mukalik and Whale Rivers are regularly traversed by the Indians, but the others are too swift and rocky for canoes. There are several streams to the westward of the Koksoak, notably Leaf River, and a very large one that the Eskimos told me of, emptying into Hope's Advance Bay, but these I did not see and my knowledge of them is limited to hearsay.

The hills in the vicinity of George River are generally high, but to the westward they are much lower and less picturesque.

After our camp was pitched we had an opportunity for the first time to make the acquaintance of our companions. The chief was a man of about forty years of age, Potokomik by name, which, translated, means a hole cut in the edge of a skin for the purpose of stretching it. The next in importance was Kumuk. Kumuk means louse, and it fitted the man's nature well. The youngest was Iksialook (Big Yolk of an Egg). Potokomik had been rechristened by a Hudson's Bay Company agent "Kenneth," and Kumuk, in like manner, had had the name of "George" bestowed upon him, but Iksialook bad been overlooked or neglected in this respect, and his brain was not taxed with trying to remember a Christian cognomen that none of his people would ever call or know him by.

Potokomik was really a remarkable man and proved most faithful to us. It is, in fact, to his faithfulness and control over the others, particularly Kumuk, that Easton and I owe our lives, as will appear later. He was at one time conjurer of the Kangerlualuksoakmiut, or George River Eskimos, and is still their leader, but during a visit to the Atlantic coast, some three or four years ago, he came under the influence of a missionary, embraced Christianity, and abandoned the heathen conjuring swindle by which he was, up to that time, making a good living. Now he lives a life about as clean and free from the heathenism and superstitions of his race as any Eskimo can who adopts a new religion. The missionary whom I have mentioned led Potokomik's mother to accept Christ and renounce Torngak when she was on her deathbed, and before she died she confessed to many sins, amongst them that of having aided in the killing and eating, when driven to the act by starvation, of her own mother.

After our tent was pitched and the Eskimos had spread the Explorer's sail as a shelter for themselves, Kumuk and Iksialook left us to look for driftwood and, in half an hour, returned with a few small sticks that they had found on the shore. These sticks were exceedingly scarce and, of course, very precious and with the greatest economy in the use of the wood, a fire was made and the kettle boiled for tea.

At first the Eskimos were always doing unexpected things and springing surprises upon us, but soon we became more or less accustomed to their ways. Not one of them could talk or understand English and my Eskimo vocabulary was limited to the one word "Oksunae," and we therefore had considerable difficulty in making each other understand, and the pantomime and various methods of communication resorted to were often very funny to see. Potokomik and I started in at once to learn what we could of each other's language, and it is wonderful how much can be accomplished in the acquirement of a vocabulary in a short time and how few words are really necessary to convey ideas. I would point at the tent and say, "Tent," and he would say, "Tupek"; or at my sheath knife and say, "Knife," and he would say, "Chevik," and thus each learned the other's word for nearly everything about us and such words as "good," "bad," "wind" and so on; and in a few days we were able to make each other understand in a general way, with our mixed English and Eskimo.

The northeast wind and low-hanging clouds of the morning carried into execution their threat, and all Sunday afternoon and all day Monday the snowstorm raged with fury. I took pity on the Eskimos and on Sunday night invited all of them to sleep in our tent, but only Potokomik came, and on Monday morning, when I went out at break of day, I found the other two sleeping under a snowdrift, for the lean-to made of the boat sail had not protected them much. After that they accepted my invitation and joined us in the tent.

It did not clear until Tuesday morning, and then we hoisted sail and started forward out of the river and into the broad, treacherous waters of Hudson Straits, working with the oars to keep warm and accelerate progress, for the wind was against us at first until we turned out of the river, and we had long tacks to make.

At the Post, as was stated, there is a rise and fall of tide of forty feet. In Ungava Bay and the straits it has a record of sixty-two feet rise at flood, with the spring or high tides, and this makes navigation precarious where hidden reefs and rocks are everywhere; and there are long stretches of coast with no friendly bay or harbor or lee shore where one can run for cover when unheralded gales and sudden squalls catch one in the open. The Atlantic coast of Labrador is dangerous indeed, but there Nature has providentially distributed innumerable safe harbor retreats, and the tide is insignificant compared with that of Ungava Bay. "Nature exhausted her supply of harbors," someone has said, "before she rounded Cape Chidley, or she forgot Ungava entirely; and she just bunched the tide in here, too."

That Tuesday night sloping rocks and ominous reefs made it impossible for us to effect a landing, and in a shallow place we dropped anchor. Fortunately there was no wind, for we were in an exposed position, and had there been we should have come to grief. A bit of hardtack with nothing to drink sufficed for supper, and after eating we curled up as best we could in the bottom of the boat. No watch was kept. Every one lay down. Easton and I rolled in our blankets, huddled close to each other, pulled the tent over us and were soon dreaming of sunnier lands where flowers bloom and the ice trust gets its prices.

Our awakening was rude. Sometime in the night I dreamed that my neck was broken and that I lay in a pool of icy water powerless to move. When I finally roused myself I found the boat tilted at an angle of forty-five degrees and my head at the lower incline. All the water in the boat had drained to that side and my shoulders and neck were immersed. The tide was out and we were stranded on the rocks. It was bright moonlight. Kumuk and Iksialook got up and with the kettle disappeared over the rocks. The rising tide was almost on us when they returned with a kettle full of hot tea. Then as soon as the water was high enough to float the boat we were off by moonlight, fastening now and again on reefs, and several times narrowly escaped disaster.

It was very cold. Easton and I were still clad in the bush-ravaged clothing that we had worn during the summer, and it was far too light to keep out the bitter Arctic winds that were now blowing, and at night our only protection was our light summer camping blankets. When we reached the Post at George River not a thing in the way of clothing or blankets was in stock and the new stores were not unpacked when we left, so we were not able to re-outfit there.

Wednesday night we succeeded in finding shelter, but all day Thursday were held prisoners by a northerly gale. On Friday we made a new start, but early in the afternoon were driven to shelter on an island, where with some difficulty we effected a landing at low tide, and carried our goods a half mile inland over the slippery rocks above the reach of rising water. The Eskimos remained with the boat and worked it in foot by foot with the tide while Easton and I pitched the tent and hunted up and down on the rocks for bits of driftwood until we had collected sufficient to last us with economy for a day or two.

That night the real winter came. The light ice that we had encountered heretofore and the snow which attained a considerable depth in the recent storms were only the harbingers of the true winter that comes in this northland with a single blast of the bitter wind from the ice fields of the Arctic. It comes in a night--almost in an hour--as it did to us now. Every pool of water on the island was congealed into a solid mass. A gale of terrific fury nearly carried our tent away, and only the big boulders to which it was anchored saved it. Once we had to shift it farther back upon the rock fields, out of reach of an exceptionally high tide. For three days the wind raged, and in those three days the great blocks of northern pack ice were swept down upon us, and we knew that the Explorer could serve us no longer. There was no alternative now but to cross the barrens to Whale River on foot. With deep snow and no snowshoes it was not a pleasant prospect.

Our hard-tack was gone, and I baked into cakes all of our little stock of flour and corn meal. This, with a small piece of pork, six pounds of pemmican, tea and a bit of tobacco was all that we had left in the way of provisions. The Eskimos had eaten everything that they had brought, and it now devolved upon us to feed them also from our meager store, which at the start only provided for Easton and me for ten days, as that had been considered more than ample time for the journey. I limited the rations at each meal to a half of one of my cakes for each man. Potokomik agreed with me that this was a wise and necessary restriction and protected me in it. Kumuk thought differently, and he was seen to filch once or twice, but a close watch was kept upon him.

With infinite labor we hauled the Explorer above the high-tide level, out of reach of the ice that would soon pile in a massive barricade of huge blocks upon the shore, that she might be safe until recovered the following spring. Then we packed in the boat's prow our tent and all paraphernalia that was not absolutely necessary for the sustenance of life, made each man a pack of his blankets, food and necessaries, and began our perilous foot march toward Whale River. I clung to all the records of the expedition, my camera, photographic films and things of that sort, though Potokomik advised their abandonment.

At low tide, when the rocks were left nearly uncovered, we forded from the island to the mainland. It was dark when we reached it, and for three hours after dark, bending under our packs, walking in Indian file, we pushed on in silence through the knee-deep snow upon which the moon, half hidden by flying clouds, cast a weird ghostlike light. Finally the Eskimos stopped in a gully by a little patch of spruce brush four or five feet high, and while Iksialook foraged for handfuls of brush that was dry enough to burn, Potokomik and Kumuk cut snow blocks, which they built into a circular wall about three feet high, as a wind-break in which to sleep, and Easton and I broke some green brush to throw upon the snow in this circular wind-break for a bed. While we did this Iksialook filled the kettle with bits of ice and melted it over his brush fire and made tea. There was only brush enough to melt ice for one cup of tea each, which with our bit of cake made our supper. . We huddled close and slept pretty well that night on the snow with nothing but flying frost between us and heaven.

We were having our breakfast the next morning a white arctic fox came within ten yards of our fire to look us over as though wondering what kind of animals we were. Easton and I were unarmed, but the Eskimos each carried a 45-90 Winchester rifle. Potokomik reached for his and shot the fox, and in a few minutes its disjointed carcass was in our pan with a bit of pork, and we made a substantial breakfast on the half-cooked flesh.

That was a weary day. We came upon a large creek in the forenoon and had to ascend its east bank for a long distance to cross it, as the tide had broken the ice below. Some distance up the stream its valley was wooded by just enough scattered spruce trees to hold the snow, and wallowing and floundering through this was most exhausting.

During the day Kumuk proposed to the other Eskimos that

they take all the food and leave the white men to their fate. They had rifles while we had none, and we could not resist. Potokomik would not hear of it. He remained our friend. Kumuk did not like the small ration that I dealt out, and if they could get the food out of our possession they would have more for themselves.

That night a snow house was built, with the exception of rounding the dome at the top, over which Potokomik spread his blanket; but it was a poor shelter, and not much warmer than the open. When I lay down I was dripping with perspiration from the exertion of the day and during the night had a severe chill.

The next day a storm threatened. We crossed another stream and halted, at twelve o'clock, upon the western side of it to make tea. The Eskimos held a consultation here and then Potokomik told us that they were afraid of heavy snow and that it was thought best to cache everything that we had--blankets, food and everything--and with nothing to encumber us hurry on to a tupek that we should reach by dark, and that there we should find shelter and food. Accordingly everything was left behind but the rifles, which the Eskimos clung to, and we started on at a terrific pace over wind-swept hills and drift-covered valleys, where all that could be seen was a white waste of unvarying snow. We had been a little distance inland, but now worked our way down toward the coast. Once we crossed an inlet where we had to climb over great blocks of ice that the tide in its force had piled there.

Just at dusk the Eskimos halted. We had reached the place where the tupek should have been, but none was there. Afterward I learned that the people whom Potokomik expected to find here had been caught on their way from Whale River by the ice and their boat was crushed.

Another consultation was held, and as a result we started on again. After a two hours' march Potokomik halted and the others left us. Easton and I threw ourselves at full length upon the snow and went to sleep on the instant. A rifle shot aroused us, and Potokomik jumped to his feet with the exclamation, "Igloo!" We followed him toward where Kumuk was shouting, through a bit of bush, down a bank, across a frozen brook and up a slope, where we found a miserable little log shack. No one was there. It was a filthy place and snow had drifted in through the openings in the roof and side. The previous occupant of the hut had left behind him an ax and an old stove, and with a few sticks of wood that we found a fire was started and we huddled close to it in a vain effort to get warm. When the fire died out we found places to lie down, and, shivering with the cold, tried with poor success to sleep.

I had another chill that night and severe cramps in the calves of my legs, and when morning came and Easton said he could not travel another twenty yards, I agreed at once to a plan of the Eskimos to leave us there while they went on to look for other Eskimos whom they expected to find in winter quarters east of Whale River. Potokomik promised to send them with dogs to our rescue and then go on with a letter to Job Edmunds, the Hudson's Bay Company's agent at Whale River. This letter to Edmunds I scribbled on a stray bit of paper I found in my pocket, and in it told him of our position, and lack of food and clothing.

Potokomik left his rifle and some cartridges with us, and then with the promise that help should find us ere we had slept three times, we shook hands with our dusky friend upon whose honor and faithfulness our lives now depended, and the three were gone in the face of a blinding snowstorm.

Shortly after the Eskimos left us we heard some ptarmigans clucking outside, and Easton knocked three of them over with Potokomik's rifle. There were four, but one got away. It can be imagined what work the .45 bullet made of them. After separating the flesh as far as possible from the feathers, we boiled it in a tin can we had found amongst the rubbish in the hut, and ate everything but the bills and toe-nails--bones, entrails and all. This, it will be remembered, was the first food that we had had since noon of the day before. We had no tea and our only comfort-providing asset was one small piece of plug tobacco.

Fortunately wood was not hard to get, but still not sufficiently plentiful for us to have more than a light fire in the stove, which we hugged pretty closely.

The storm grew in fury. It shrieked around our poorly built shack, drifting the snow in through the holes and crevices until we could not find a place to sit or lie that was free from it. On the night of the third day the weather cleared and settled, cold and rasping. I took the rifle and looked about for game, but the snow was now so deep that walking far in it was out of the question. I did not see the track or sign of any living thing save a single whisky-jack, but even he was shy and kept well out of range.

We had nothing to eat--not a mouthful of anything--and only water to drink; even our tobacco was soon gone. Day after day we sat, sometimes in silence, for hours at a time, sometimes calculating upon the probabilities of the Eskimos having perished in the storm, for they were wholly without protection. I had faith in Potokomik and his resourcefulness, and was hopeful they would get out safely. If there had been timber in the country where night shelter could be made, we might have started for Whale River without further delay. But in the wide waste barrens, inadequately clothed, with deep snow to wallow through, it seemed to me absolutely certain that such an attempt would end in exhaustion and death, so we restrained our impatience and waited. On scraps of paper we played tit-tat-toe; we improvised a checkerboard and played checkers. These pastimes broke the monotony of waiting somewhat. No matter what we talked about, our conversation always drifted to something to eat. We planned sumptuous banquets we were to have at that uncertain period "when we get home," discussing in the minutest detail each dish. Once or twice Easton roused me in the night to ask whether after all some other roast or soup had not better be selected than the one we had decided upon, or to suggest a change in vegetables.

We slept five times instead of thrice and still no succor came. The days were short, the nights interminably long. I knew we could live for twelve or fifteen days easily on water. I had recovered entirely from the chills and cramps and we were both feeling well but, of course, rather weak. We had lost no flesh to speak of. The extreme hunger had passed away after a couple of days. It is only when starving people have a little to eat that the hunger period lasts longer than that. Novelists write a lot of nonsense about the pangs of hunger and the extreme suffering that accompanies starvation. It is all poppycock. Any healthy person, with a normal appetite, after missing two or three meals is as hungry as he ever gets. After awhile there is a sense of weakness that grows on one, and this increases with the days. Then there comes a desire for a great deal of sleep, a sort of lassitude that is not unpleasant, and this desire becomes more pronounced as the weakness grows. The end is always in sleep. There is no keeping awake until the hour of death.

While, as I have said, the real sense of hunger passes away quickly there remains the instinct to eat. That is the working of the first law of nature--self-preservation. It prompts one to eat anything that one can chew or swallow, and it is what makes men eat refuse the thought of which would sicken them at other times. Of course, Easton and I were like everybody else under similar conditions. Easton said one day that he would like to have something to chew on. In the refuse on the floor I found a piece of deerskin about ten inches square. I singed the hair off of it and divided it equally between us and then we each roasted our share and ate it. That was the evening after we had "slept" five times.

After disposing of our bit of deerskin we huddled down on the floor with our heads pillowed upon sticks of wood, as was our custom, for a sixth night, after discussing again the probable fate of the Eskimos. While I did not admit to Easton that I entertained any doubt as to our ultimate rescue, as the days passed and no relief came I felt grave fears as to the safety of Potokomik and his companions. The severe storm that swept over the country after their departure from the shack had no doubt materially deepened the snow, and I questioned whether or not this had made it impossible for them to travel without snowshoes. The wind during the second day of the storm had been heavy, and it was my hope that it had swept the barrens clear of the new snow, but this was uncertain and doubtful. Then, too, I did not know the nature of Eskimos--whether they were wont to give up quickly in the face of unusual privations and difficulties such as these men would have to encounter. They were in a barren country, with no food, no blankets, no tent, no protection, in fact, of any kind from the elements, and it was doubtful whether they would find material for a fire at night to keep them from freezing, and, even if they did find wood, they had no ax with which to cut it. How far they would have to travel surrounded by these conditions I had no idea. Indians without wood or food or a sheltering bush would soon give up the fight and lie down to die. If Potokomik and his men had perished, I knew that Easton and I could hope for no relief from the outside and that our salvation would depend entirely upon our own resourcefulness. It seemed to me the time had come when some action must be taken.

It was a long while after dark, I do not know how long, and I still lay awake turning these things over in my mind, when I heard a strange sound. Everything had been deathly quiet for days, and I sat up. In the great unbroken silence of the wilderness a man's fancy will make him hear strange things. I have answered the shouts of men that my imagination made me hear. But this was not fancy, for I heard it again--a distinct shout! I jumped to my feet and called to Easton: "They've come, boy! Get up, there's someone coming!" Then I hurried outside and, in the dim light on the white stretch of snow, saw a black patch of men and dogs. Our rescuers had come.

Chapter 17: To Whale River and Fort Chimo

The feeling of relief that came to me when I heard the shout and saw the men and dogs coming can be appreciated, and something of the satisfaction I felt when I grasped the hands of the two Eskimos that strode up on snowshoes can be understood.

The older of the two was an active little fellow who looked much like a Japanese. He introduced himself as Emuk (Water). His companion, who, we learned later, rejoiced in the name Amnatuhinuk (Only a Woman), was quite a young fellow, big, fat and good-natured.

Without any preliminaries Emuk pushed right into the shack and, from a bag that he carried, produced some tough dough cakes which he gave us to eat, and each a plug of tobacco to smoke. He was all activity and command, working quickly himself and directing Amnatuhinuk. A candle from his bag was lighted. Amnatuhinuk was sent for a kettle of water; wood was piled into the stove, and the kettle put over to boil. The stove proved too slow for Emuk and he built a fire outside where tea could be made more quickly, and when it was ready he insisted upon our drinking several cups of it to stimulate us. Then he brought forth a pail containing strong-smelling beans cooked in rancid seal oil, which he heated. This concoction he thought was good strong food and just the thing for half-starved men, and he set it before us with the air of one who has done something especially nice. We ate some of it but were as temperate as Emuk with his urgings would permit us to be, for I knew the penalty that food exacts after a long fast.

A comfortable bed of boughs and blankets was spread for us,

and we were made to lie down. Emuk, on more than one occasion, bad been in a similar position to ours and others had come to his aid, and he wanted to pay the debt he felt he owed to humanity.

He told us that Potokomik and the others, after suffering great hardships, had reached his tupek near the Mukalik the day before, but I could not understand his language well enough to draw from him any of the details of their trip out.

At midnight Emuk made tea again and roused us up to partake of it and eat more dough cakes and beans with seal oil. I feared the consequences, but I could not refuse him, for he did not understand why we should not want to eat a great deal. The result was that with happiness and stomach ache I could not sleep, and before morning was going out to vomit. Even at the danger of seeming not to appreciate Emuk's hospitality, I was constrained to decline to eat any breakfast.

Emuk noticed a hole in the bottom of one of my seal-skin boots. He promptly pulled off his own and made me put them on. He had another though poorer pair for himself.

It was a delight to be moving again. We were on the trail before dawn, Emuk with his snowshoes tramping the road ahead of the dogs and Amnatuhinuk driving the team. The temperature must have been at least ten degrees below zero. The weather was bitterly cold for men so thinly clad as Easton and I were, and the snow was so deep that we could not exercise by running, for we had no snowshoes, and while we wallowed through the deep snow the dogs would have left us behind, so we could do nothing but sit on the komatik (sledge) and shiver.

At noon we stopped at the foot of a hill before ascending it, and the men threw up a wind-break of snow blocks, back of which they built a fire and put over the teakettle. Easton and I had just squatted close to the fire to warm our benumbed hands when the husky dogs put their noses in the air and gave out the long weird howl of welcome or defiance that announces the approach of other dogs, and almost immediately a loaded team with two men came over the hill and down the slope at a gallop toward us. It proved to be Job Edmunds, the half- breed Hudson's Bay Company officer from Whale River, and his Eskimo servant, coming to our aid.

Edmunds was greatly relieved to find us safe. He knew exactly what to do. From his komatik box he produced a bottle of port wine and made us each take a small dose of it which he poured into a tin cup. He put a big, warm reindeer-skin koolutuk [the outer garment of deerskin worn by the Eskimos] on each of us and pulled the hoods over our heads. He had warm footwear--in fact, everything that was necessary for our comfort. Then he cut two ample slices of wheat bread from a big loaf, and toasted and buttered them for us. He was very kind and considerate. Edmunds has saved many lives in his day. Every winter he is called upon to go to the rescue of Eskimos who have been caught in the barrens without food, as we were. He had saved Emuk from starvation on one or two occasions.

After a half-hour's delay we were off again, I on the komatik with Edmunds, and Easton with Emuk. We passed the snow house where Edmunds and his man had spent the previous night. They would have come on in the dark, but they knew Emuk was ahead and would reach us anyway.

Edmunds had a splendid team of dogs, wonderfully trained. The big, wolfish creatures loved him and they feared him. He almost never had to use the long walrus-hide whip. They obeyed him on the instant without hesitation--"Ooisht," and they pulled in the harness as one; "Aw," and they stopped. There was a power in his voice that governed them like magic. The wind had packed the snow hard enough on the barrens beyond the Tuktotuk--and the country there was all barren--to bear up the komatik; the dogs were in prime condition and traveled at a fast trot or a gallop, and we made good time. Once Emuk stopped to take a white fox out of a trap. He killed it by pressing his knee on its breast and stifling its heart beats.

Big cakes of ice were piled in high barricades along the rivers where we crossed them, and at these places we had to let the komatik down with care on one side and help the dogs haul it up with much labor on the other; and on the level, through the rough ice hummocks or amongst the rocks, the drivers were kept busy steering to prevent collisions with the obstructions, while the dogs rushed madly ahead, and we, on the komatik, clung on for dear life and watched our legs that they might not get crushed. Once or twice we turned over, but the drivers never lost their hold of the komatik or control of the dogs.

It was dark when we reached Emuk's skin tupek and were welcomed by a group of Eskimos, men, women and children. Iksialook was of the number, and he was so worn and haggard that I scarcely recognized him. He had seen hardship since our parting. The people were very dirty and very hospitable. They took us into the tupek at once, which was extremely filthy and made insufferably hot by a sheet-iron tent stove. The women wore sealskin trousers and in the long hoods of their adikeys, or upper garments, carried babies whose bright little dusky-hued faces peeped timidly out at us over the mothers' shoulders. A ptarmigan was boiled and divided between Easton and me, and with that and bread and butter from Edmunds's box and hot tea we made a splendid supper. After a smoke all around, for the women smoke as well as the men, polar bear and reindeer skins were spread upon spruce boughs, blankets were given us for covering, and we lay down. Eleven of us crowded into the tupek and slept there that night. How all the Eskimos found room I do not know. I was crowded so tightly between one of the fat women on one side and Easton on the other that I could not turn over; but I slept as I had seldom ever slept before.

The next forenoon we crossed the Mukalik River and soon after reached Whale River, big and broad, with blocks of ice surging up and down upon the bosom of the restless tide. The Post is about ten miles from its mouth. We turned northward along its east bank and, in a little while, came to some scattered spruce woods, which Edmunds told me were just below his home. Then at a creek, above which stood the miniature log cabin and small log storehouse comprising the Post buildings, I got off and climbed up through rough ice barricades.

Never in my life have I had such a welcome as I received here. Mrs. Edmunds came out to meet me. She told me that they had been watching for us at the Post all the morning and how glad they were that we were safe, and that we had come to see them, and that we must stay a good long time and rest. For two-score years they had lived in that desolate place and never before had a traveler come to visit them. In all that time the only white people they had ever met were the three or four connected with the Post at Fort Chimo, for the ship never calls at Whale River on her rounds. Edmunds brings the provisions over from Fort Chimo in a little schooner. There are five in the family--Edmunds and his wife, their daughter (a young woman of twenty) and her husband, Sam Ford (a son of John Ford at George River), and Mary's baby.

A good wash and clean clothing followed by a sumptuous dinner of venison put us on our feet again. I suffered little as a result of the fasting period, but Easton had three or four days of pretty severe colic. This is the usual result of feast after famine, and was to be expected.

And now I learned the details of Potokomik's journey out. When the three Eskimos left us in the shack they started at once in search of Emuk's tupek. The storm that raged for two days swept pitilessly across their path, but they never halted, pushing through the deepening snow in single file, taking turns at going ahead and breaking the way, until night, and then they stopped. They had no ax and could have no fire, so they built themselves a snow igloo as best they could without the proper implements and it protected them against the drifting snow and piercing wind while they slept. On the second day they shot, with their rifles, seven ptarmigans. These they plucked and ate raw. They saw no more game, and finally became so weak and exhausted they could carry their rifles no farther and left them on the trail. Each night they built a snow house. With increasing weakness their progress was very slow; still they kept going, staggering on and on through the snow. It was only their lifelong habit of facing great odds and enduring great hardships that kept them up. Men less inured to cold and privation would surely have succumbed. They were making their final fight when at last they stumbled into Emuk's tupek. Kumuk sat down and cried like a child. It was two weeks before any of them was able to do any physical work. They looked like shadows of their former selves when I saw them at Whale River.

It was after dark Sunday night when my letter to Edmunds reached the Post. Earlier in the evening Edmunds and his man had crossed the river, which is here over half a mile in width, and pitched their camp on the opposite shore, preparatory to starting up the river the next morning on a deer hunt, herds having been reported to the northward by Eskimos. Mrs. Edmunds read the letter, and she and Mary were at once all excitement. They lighted a lantern and signaled to the camp on the other side and fired guns until they had a reply. Then, for fear that Edmunds might not understand the urgency of his immediate returns they kept firing at intervals all night, stopping only to pack the komatik box with the clothing and food that Edmunds was to bring to us. Neither of the women slept. With the thought of men starving out in the snow they could not rest. The floating ice in the river and the swift tide made it impossible for a boat to cross in the darkness, but with daylight Edmunds returned, harnessed his dogs, and was off to meet us as has been described.

We had left George River on October twenty-second, and it was the eighth of November when we reached Whale River, and in this interval the caribou herds that the Indians had reported west of the Koksoak had passed to the east of Whale River and turned to the northward. Fifty miles inland the Indian and Eskimo hunters had met them. The killing was over and they told us hundreds of the animals lay dead in the snow above. So many had been butchered that all the dogs and men in Ungava would be well supplied with meat during the winter, and numbers of the carcasses would feed the packs of timber wolves that infested the country or rot in the next summer's sun. Sam Ford had gone inland but was too late for the big hunt and only killed four or five deer. The wolves were so thick, he told us, that he could not sleep at night in his camp with the noise of their howling. One Eskimo brought in two wolf skins that were so large when they were stretched a man could almost have crawled into either of them. I saw wolf tracks myself within a quarter mile of the Post, for the animals were so bold they ventured almost to the door.

Edmunds is a famous hunter. During the previous winter, besides attending to his post duties, he killed nearly half a hundred caribou to supply his Post and Fort Chimo with man and dog food, and in the same season his traps yielded him two hundred fox pelts--mostly white ones--his personal catch. This was not an unusual year's work for him. Mary inherits her father's hunting instincts. In the morning she would put her baby in the hood of her adikey, shoulder her gun, don her snowshoes, and go to "tend" her traps. One day she did not take her gun, and when she had made her rounds of the traps and started homeward discovered that she was being followed by a big gray timber wolf. When she stopped, the wolf stopped; when she went on, it followed, stealing gradually closer and closer to her, almost imperceptibly, but still gaining upon her. She wanted to run, but she realized that if she did the wolf would know at once that she was afraid and would attack and kill her and her baby; so without hastening her pace, and only looking back now and again to note the wolf's gain, she reached the door of the house and entered with the animal not ten paces away. Now she always carries a gun and feels no fear, for she can shoot.

I took advantage of the delay at Whale River to partially outfit for the winter. Edmunds and his family rendered us valuable assistance and advice, securing for us, from the Eskimos, sealskin boots, and from the Indians who came to the Post while we were there, deer skins for trousers, koolutuks and sleeping bags, Mrs. Edmunds and Mary themselves making our moccasins, mittens and duffel socks.

The Eskimos were all away at their hunting grounds and it was not possible to secure a dog team to carry us on to Fort Chimo. Therefore, when Edmunds announced one day that he must send Sam Ford and the Eskimo servant over with the Post team for a load of provisions, I availed myself of the opportunity to accompany them, and on the twenty-eighth of November we said good-by to the friends who had been so kind to us and again faced toward the westward.

The morning was clear, crisp and bracing; the temperature was twenty degrees below zero. We ascended the river some seven or eight miles before we found a safe crossing, as the tide had kept the ice broken in the center of the channel below, and piled it like hills along the banks.

I noted that the Whale River valley was much better wooded than any country we had seen for a long time--since we had left the head waters of the George River, in fact--and the Indians say it is so to its source. The trees are small black spruce and larch, but a fairly thick growth. This "bush," however, is evidently quite restricted in width, for after crossing the river we were almost immediately out of it, and the same interminable, barren, rocky, treeless country that we had seen to the eastward extended westward to the Koksoak.

140

That night was spent in a snow igloo. The next day we crossed the False River, a wide stream at its mouth, but a little way up not over two hundred yards wide. At twelve o'clock a halt was made at an Eskimo tupek for dinner.

The people were, as these northern people always are, most hospitable, giving us the best they had--fresh venison and tea. After but an hour's delay we were away again, and at three o'clock, with the dogs on a gallop, rounded the hill above Fort Chimo and pulled into the Post, the farthest limit of white man's habitation in all Labrador.

We were welcomed by Mr. Duncan Mathewson, the Chief Trader, who has charge of the Ungava District for the Hudson's Bay Company, and Dr. Alexander Milne, Assistant Commissioner of the Company, from Winnipeg, who had arrived on the Pelican and was on a tour of inspection of the Labrador Coast Posts.

The Chief Trader's residence is a small building, and Mr. Mathewson was unable to entertain us in the house, but he gave orders at once to have a commodious room in one of the dozen or so other buildings of the Post fitted up for us with beds, stove and such simple furnishings as were necessary to establish us in housekeeping and make us comfortable during our stay with him. Here we were to remain until the Indian and Eskimo hunters came for their Christmas and New Year's trading, at which time, I was advised, I should probably be able to engage Eskimo drivers and dogs to carry us eastward to the Atlantic coast.

Chapter 18: The Indians of the North

Fort Chmio is situated upon the east bank of the Koksoak River and about twenty-five miles from its mouth, where the river is nearly a mile and a half wide. There are two trading posts here; one, that of the Hudson's Bay Company, consisting of a dozen or so buildings, which include dwelling and storehouses and native cabins; the other that of Revellion Brothers, the great fur house of Paris, colloquially referred to as "the French Company," which stands just above and ad- joining the station of the Hudson's Bay Company. This latter Post was erected in the year 1903, and has nearly as many buildings as the older establishment. We used to refer to them respectively as "London" and "Paris."

The history of Fort Chimo extends back to the year 1811, when Kmoch and Kohlmeister, two of the Moravian Brethren of the Okak Mission on the Atlantic coast, in the course of their efforts for the conversion of the Eskimos to Christianity cruised into Ungava Bay, discovered the George River, which they named in honor of King George the Third, and then proceeded to the Koksoak, which they ascended to the point of the present settlement. The natives received them well. They erected a beacon on a hill, tarried but a few days and then turned back to Okak. Upon their return they gave glowing accounts of their reception by the natives and the great possibilities for profitable trade, but they did not deem it advisable themselves to extend their labors to that field.

In the course of time this report drifted to England and to the ears of the officials of the Hudson's Bay Company, who were attracted by it, and in 1827 Dr. Mendry, an officer of the

Company at Moose Factory, with a party of white men and Indian guides crossed the peninsula from Richmond Gulf, through Clearwater Lake to the head waters of the Larch River, a tributary of the Koksoak, thence descended the Larch and Koksoak to the place where the Moravians had erected the beacon, and on a low terrace, just across the river from the beacon, established the original Fort Chimo. The difficulties of navigation and the consequent uncertainty and expense of keeping the Post supplied with provisions and articles of trade were such, however, that after a brief trial Ungava was abandoned.

The opportunities for lucrative trade here were not forgotten by the Company, and in the year 1837 Factor John McLean was detailed to re- establish Fort Chimo. This he did, and a year later built the first Post at George River. During the succeeding winter he crossed the interior with dogs to Northwest River. Upon their return journey McLean and his party ate their dogs and barely escaped perishing from starvation; one of his Indians, who was sent ahead, reaching Fort Chimo and bringing succor when McLean and the others, through extreme weakness, were unable to proceed farther. In the following summer McLean built the fort on Indian House Lake, and the other one that has been mentioned, on a large lake to the westward--Lake Eraldson he called it--presumably the source of Whale River. Later he succeeded in crossing to Northwest River by canoe, ascending the George River and descending the Atlantic slope of the plateau by way of the Grand River. His object was to establish a regular line of communication between Fort Chimo and Northwest River, with interior posts along the route. The natural obstacles which the country presented finally forced the abandonment of this plan as impracticable, and the two interior posts were closed after a brief trial. This was before the days of steam navigation, and with sailing vessels it was only possible to reach these isolated northern stations in Ungava Bay with supplies once every two years. Even these infrequent visits were so fraught with danger and uncertainty that finally, in 1855, Fort Chimo and George River were again abandoned as unprofitable. In 1866, however, the building of the Company's steamship Labrador made yearly visits possible, and in that year another attack was made upon the Ungava district and Fort Chimo was rebuilt, George River Post re- established, and a little later the small station at Whale River was erected. With the improved facilities for transportation the trade with Indians and Eskimos, and the salmon and white whale fisheries carried on by the Posts, now proved most profitable, and the Company has since and is still reaping the reward of its persistence.

Dr. Milne, as has been stated, was not a permanent resident of the Post. Regularly stationed here, besides Mathewson, there is a young clerk, a cooper, a carpenter, and a handy man, all Scotchmen, and a comparatively new arrival, Rev. Samuel M. Stewart, a missionary of the Church Mission Society of England. Of Mr. Stewart, who did much to relieve the monotony of our several weeks' sojourn at Fort Chimo, and his remarkable self-sacrifice and work, I shall have something to say later.

The day after our arrival we took occasion to pay our respects to Monsieur D. The'venet, the officer in charge of the "French Post." Our reception was most cordial. M. The'venet is a gentleman by birth. He was at one time an officer in the French cavalry, but his love of adventure and active temperament rebelled against the inactivity of garrison duty and he resigned his commission in the army, came to Canada, and joined the Northwest mounted police in the hope of obtaining a detail in the Klondike. In this he was disappointed, and the outbreak of the South African war offering a new field of adventure he quit the police, enlisted in the Canadian Mounted Rifles, and served in the field throughout the war. After his return to Canada and discharge from the army, he took service with Revellion Brothers.

M. The'venet invited us to dine with him that very evening, and we were not slow to accept his hospitality. His bright conversation, pleasing personality and unstinted hospitality offered a delightful evening and we were not disappointed. This and many other pleasant evenings spent in his society during our stay at Fort Chimo were some of the most enjoyable of our trip.

Here an agreeable surprise awaited me. When we sat down to dinner The'venet called in his new half-breed French-Indian interpreter, and who should he prove to be but Belfleur, one of

144

the dog drivers who in April, 1904, accompanied me from Northwest River to Rigolet, when I began that anxious journey over the ice with Hubbard's body. He was apparently as well pleased at the meeting as I. Belfleur and a half- breed Scotch-Eskimo named Saunders are employed as Indian and Eskimo interpreters at the French Post, and are the only ones of M. The'venet's people with whom he can converse. Belfleur speaks French and broken English, and Saunders English, besides their native languages.

None of the people of Ungava, with the exception of two or three, speaks any but his mother tongue, and they have no ambition, apparently, to extend their linguistic acquirements. It is, indeed, a lonely life for the trader, who but once a year, when his ship arrives, has any communication with the great world which he has left behind him. No white woman is here with her softening influence, no physician or surgeon to treat the sick and injured, and never until the advent of Mr. Stewart any permanent missionary.

The natives that remain at Fort Chimo all the year are three or four families of Eskimos, a few old or crippled Indians, and some half- breed Indians and Eskimos, who do chores around the Posts and lead an uncertain existence. The half-breed Indian children are taken care of at the "Indian house," a log structure presided over by the "Queen" of Ungava, a very corpulent old Nascaupee woman, who lives by the labor of others and draws tribute from trading Indians who make the Indian house their rendezvous when they visit the Post. She is and always has been very kind, and a sort of mother, to the little waifs that nearly every trader or white servant has left behind him, when the Company's orders transferred him to some other Post and he abandoned his temporary wife forever.

The Indians of the Ungava district are chiefly Nascaupees, with occasionally a few Crees from the West. "Nenenot" they call themselves, which means perfect, true men. "Nascaupee" means false or untrue men and is a word of opprobrium applied to them by the Mountaineers in the early days, because of their failure to keep a compact to join forces with the latter at the time of the wars for supremacy between the Indians and Eskimos. Nascaupee is the name by which they are known now, outside of their own lodges, and the one which we shall use in referring to them. In like manner I have chosen to use the English Mountaineer, rather than the French Montagnais, in speaking of the southern Indians. North of the Straits of Belle Isle the French word is never heard, and if you were to refer to these Indians as "Montagnais" to the Labrador natives it is doubtful whether you would be understood.

Both Mountaineers and Nascaupees are of Cree origin, and belong to the great Algonquin family. Their language is similar, with only the variation of dialect that might be expected with the different environments. The Nascaupees have one peculiarity of speech, however, which is decidedly their own. In conversation their voice is raised to a high pitch, or assumes a whining, petulant tone. An outsider might believe them to be quarreling and highly excited, when in fact they are on the best of terms and discussing some ordinary subject in a most matter of fact way.

In personal appearance the Nascaupees are taller and more angular than their southern brothers, but the high cheek bones, the color and general features are the same. They are capable of enduring the severest cold. In summer cloth clothing obtained in barter at the Posts is, worn, but in winter deerskin garments are usual. The coat has the hair inside, and the outside of the finely dressed, chamoislike skin is decorated with various designs in color, in startling combinations of blue, red and yellow, painted on with dyes obtained at the Post or manufactured by themselves from fish roe and mineral products. When the garment has a hood it is sometimes the skin of a wolf's head, with the ears standing and hair outside, giving the wearer a startling and ferocious appearance. Tight-fitting deerskin or red cloth leggings decorated with beads, and deerskin moccasins complete the costume.

Some beadwork trimming is made by the women, but they do little in the way of needlework embroidery, and the results of their attempts in this direction are very indifferent. This applies to the full-blood Nascaupees. I have seen some fairly good specimens of moccasin embroidery done by the half-breed women at the Post, and by the Mountaineer women in the South.

The Nascaupees are not nearly so clean nor so prosperous as the Mountaineers, and, coming very little in contact with the whites, live now practically as their forefathers lived for untold generations before them--just as they lived, in fact, before the white men came. They are perhaps the most primitive Indians on the North American continent to-day.

The Mountaineers, on the other hand, see much more, particularly during the summer months, of the whites and half-breeds of the coast. Most of those who spend their summers on the St. Lawrence, west of St. Augustine, have more or less white blood in their veins through consorting with the traders and settlers. With but two or three exceptions the Mountaineers of the Atlantic coast, Groswater Bay, and at St. Augustine and the eastward, are pure, uncontaminated Indians.

The line of territorial division between the Nascaupee and Mountaineer Indians' hunting grounds is pretty closely drawn. The divide north of Lake Michikamau is the southern and the George River the eastern boundary of the Nascaupee territory, and to the south and to the east of these boundaries, lie the hunting grounds of the Mountaineers.

These latter, south of the height of land, as has been stated, are practically all under the influence of the Roman Catholic Church, and are most devout in the observance of their religious obligations. While it is true that their faith is leavened to some extent by the superstitions that their ancestors have handed down to them, yet even in the long months of the winter hunting season they never forget the teachings of their father confessor.

The Nascaupees are heathens. About the year 1877 or 1878 Father P'ere Lacasse crossed overland from Northwest River, apparently by the Grand River route, to Fort Chimo, in an attempt to carry the work of the mission into that field. The Nascaupees, however, did not take kindly to the new religion, and unfortunately during the priest's stay among them, which was brief, the hunting was bad. This was attributed to the missionary's presence, and the sachems were kept busy for a time dispelling the evil charm. No one was converted. Let us hope that Mr. Stewart, who is there to stay, and is an earnest, persistent worker, will reach the savage confidence and conscience, though his opportunity with the Indians is small, for these Nascaupees tarry but a very brief time each year within his reach. With open water in the summer they come to the Fort with the pelts of their winter catch. These are exchanged for arms, ammunition, knives, clothing, tea and tobacco, chiefly. Then, after a short rest they disappear again into the fastnesses of the wilderness above, to fish the interior lakes and hunt the forests, and no more is seen of them until the following summer, excepting only a few of the younger men who usually emerge from the silent, snow-bound land during Christmas week to barter skins for such necessaries as they are in urgent need of, and to get drunk on a sort of beer, a concoction of hops, molasses and unknown ingredients, that the Post dwellers make and the "Queen" dispenses during the holiday festivals.

Reindeer, together with ptarmigans (Arctic grouse) and fish, form their chief food supply, with tea always when they can get it. All of these northern Indiana are passionately fond of tea, and drink unbelievable quantities of it. Little flour is used. The deer are erratic in their movements and can never be depended upon with any degree of certainty, and should the Indians fail in their hunt they are placed face to face with starvation, as was the case in the winter of 1892 and 1893, when full half of the people perished from lack of food.

Formerly the migrating herds pretty regularly crossed the Koksoak very near and just above the Post in their passage to the eastward in the early autumn, but for several years now only small bands have been seen here, the Indians meeting the deer usually some forty or fifty miles farther up the river. When the animals swim the river they bunch close together; Indian canoe men head them off and turn them up- stream, others attacking the helpless animals with spears. An agent of the Hudson's Bay Company told me that he had seen nearly four hundred animals slaughtered in this manner in a few hours. When bands of caribou are met in winter they are driven into deep snow banks, and, unable to help themselves, are speared at will.

Of course when the killing is a large one the flesh of all the animals cannot be preserved, and frequently only the tongues are used. Of late years, however, owing to the growing scarcity of reindeer, it is said the Indians have learned to be a little less wasteful than formerly, and to restrict their kill more nearly to their needs, though during the winter I was there hundreds were slaughtered for tongues and sinew alone. Large quantities of the venison are dried and stored up against a season of paucity. Pemmican, which was formerly so largely used by our western Indians, is occasionally though not generally made by those of Labrador. When deer are killed some bone, usually a shoulder blade, is hung in a tree as an offering to the Manitou, that he may not interfere with future hunts, and drive the animals away.

The Indian religion is not one of worship, but one of fear and superstition. They are constantly in dread of imaginary spirits that haunt the wilderness and drive away the game or bring sickness or other disaster upon them. The conjurer is employed to work his charms to keep off the evil ones. They evidently have some sort of indefinite belief in a future existence, and hunting implements and other offerings are left with the dead, who, where the conditions will permit, are buried in the ground.

Sometimes the very old people are abandoned and left to die of starvation unattended. Be it said to the honor of the trading companies that they do their utmost to prevent this when it is possible, and offer the old and decrepit a haven at the Post, where they are fed and cared for.

The marriage relation is held very lightly and continence and chastity are not in their sight virtues. A child born to an unmarried woman is no impediment to her marriage. If it is a male child it is, in fact, an advantage. Love does not enter into the Indian's marriage relationship. It is a mating for convenience. Gifts are made to the girl's father or nearest male relative, and she is turned over, whether she will or no, to the would-be husband. There is no ceremony. A hunter has as many wives as he is physically able to control and take care of-- one, two or even three. Sometimes it happens that they combine against him and he receives at their hands what is doubtless well-merited chastisement.

The men are the hunters, the women the slaves. No one finds fault with this, not even the women, for it is an Indian custom immemorial for the woman to do all the hard, physical work.

The Mountaineer Indians that we met on the George River, and one Indian who visited Fort Chimo while we were there, are the only ones of the Labrador that I have ever seen drive dogs. This Fort Chimo Indian, unlike the other hunters of his people, has spent much time at the Post, and mingled much with the white traders and the Eskimos, and, for an Indian, entertains very progressive and broad views. He was, with the exception of a humpbacked post attache' who had an Eskimo wife, the only Indian I met that would not be insulted when one addressed him in Eskimo, for the Indians and Eskimos carry on no social intercourse and the Indians rather despise the Eskimos. The Indian referred to, however, has learned something of the Eskimo language, and also a little English--English that you cannot always understand, but must take for granted. He informed me, "Me three man--Indian, husky (Eskimo), white man." He was very proud of his accomplishments.

The Indian hauls his loads in winter on toboggans, which he manufactures himself with his ax and crooked knife--the only woodworking tools he possesses. The crooked knives he makes, too, from old files, shaping and tempering them.

The snowshoe frames are made by the men, the babiche is cut and netted by the women, who display wonderful skill in this work. The Mountaineers make much finer netted snowshoes than the Nascaupees, and have great pride in the really beautiful, light snowshoes that they make. No finer ones are to be found anywhere than those made by the Groswater Bay Mountaineers. Three shapes are in vogue--the beaver tail, the egg tail and the long tail. The beaver-tail snowshoes are much more difficult to make, and are seldom seen amongst the Nascaupees. With them the egg tail is the favorite.

The Ungava Indians never go to the open bay in their canoes. They have a superstition that it will bring them bad luck, for there they say the evil spirits dwell. Of all the Indians that visit Fort Chimo only two or three have ever ventured to look upon the waters of Ungava Bay, and these had their view from a hilltop at a safe distance.

It is safe to say that there is not a truthful Indian in Labrador. In fact it is considered an accomplishment to lie cheerfully and well. They are like the Crees of James Bay and the westward in this respect, and will lie most plausibly when it will serve their purpose better than truth, and I verily believe these Indians sometimes lie for the mere pleasure of it when it might be to their advantage to tell the truth.

One good and crowning characteristic these children of the

Ungava wilderness possess--that of honesty. They will not steal. You may have absolute confidence in them in this respect. And I may say, too, that they are most hospitable to the traveler, as our own experience with them exemplified. For their faults they must not be condemned. They live according to their lights, and their lights are those of the untutored savage who has never heard the gospel of Christianity and knows nothing of the civilization of the great world outside. Their life is one of constant struggle for bare existence, and it is truly wonderful how they survive at all in the bleak wastes which they inhabit.

NOTE.--It must not be supposed that all of the statements made in this chapter with reference to the Indian, particularly the Nascaupees, are the result of my personal observations. During our brief stay at Ungava, much of this information was gleaned from the officers of the two trading companies, and from natives. In a number of instances they were verified by myself, but I have taken the liberty, when doubt or conflicting statements existed, of referring to the works of Mr. A. P. Low of the Canadian Geological Society and Mr. Lucien M. Turner of the Bureau of Ethnology at Washington, to set myself right.

Chapter 19: The Eskimos of Labrador

During our stay in Ungava, and the succeeding weeks while we traveled down the ice-bound coast, we were brought into constant and intimate contact with the Eskimos. We saw them in almost every phase of their winter life, eating and sleeping with them in their tupeks and igloos, and meeting them in their hunting camps and at the Fort, when they came to barter and to enjoy the festivities of the Christmas holiday week.

The Cree Indians used to call these people "Ashkimai," which means "raw meat eaters," and it is from this appellation that our word Eskimo is derived. Here in Ungava and on the coast of Hudson's Bay, they are pretty generally known as "Huskies," a contraction of "Huskimos," the pronunciation given to the word Eskimos by the English sailors of the trading vessels, with their well-known penchant for tacking on the "h" where it does not belong, and leaving it off when it should be pronounced.

The Eskimos call themselves "Innuit," [Singular, Innuk; dual, Innuek] which means people--humans. The white visitor is a "Kablunak," or outlander, while a breed born in the country is a "Kablunangayok," or one partaking of the qualities of both the Innuk and the Kablunak. Those who live in the Koksoak district are called "Koksoagmiut," * and those of the George River district are the "Kangerlualuksoagmiut." **

The ethnologists, I believe, have never agreed upon the origin of the Eskimo, some claiming it is Mongolian, some otherwise. In passing I shall simply remark that in appearance they certainly resemble the Mongolian race. If some of the men that I saw in the North were dressed like Japanese or Chinese and placed side by side with them, the one could not be told from the other so long as the Eskimos kept their mouths closed.

In our old school geographies we used to see them pictured as stockily built little fellows. In real life they compare well in stature with the white man of the temperate zone. With a very few exceptions the Eskimos of Ungava average over five feet eight inches in height, with some six-footers.

* Kok, river; soak, big; miut, inhabitants; Koksoagmiut, inhabitants of the big river.

** Literally, inhabitants of the very big bay. The George River mouth widens into a bay which is known as the Very Big Bay.

Their legs are shorter and their bodies longer than the white man's, and this probably is one reason why they have such wonderful capacity for physical endurance. In this respect they are the superior of the Indian. With plenty of food and a bush to lie under at night the Indian will doubtless travel farther in a given time than the Eskimo. But turn them both loose with only food enough for one meal a day for a month on the bare rocks or ice fields of the Arctic North, and your Indian will soon be dead, while your Eskimo will emerge from the test practically none the worse for his experience, for it is a usual experience with him and he has a wonderful amount of dogged perseverance. The Eskimo knows better how to husband his food than the Indian; and give him a snow bank and he can make himself comfortable anywhere. The most gluttonous Indian would turn green with envy to see the quantities of meat the Eskimo can stow away within his inner self at a single sitting; but on the other hand he can live, and work hard too, on a single scant meal a day, just as his dogs do.

The facial characteristics of the Eskimo are wide cheek bones and round, full face, with a flat, broad nose. I used to look at these flat, comfortable noses on very cold days and wish that for winter travel I might be able to exchange the longer face projection that my Scotch-Irish forbears have handed down to me for one of them, for they are not so easily frosted in a forty or fifty degrees below zero temperature. By the way, if you ever get your nose frozen do not rub snow on it. If you do you will rub all the skin off, and have a pretty sore member to nurse for some time afterward. Grasp it, instead, in your bare hand. That is the Eskimo's way, and he knows. My advice is founded upon experience.

They are not so dark-hued as the Indians--in fact, many of them are no darker than the average white man under like conditions of exposure to wind and storm and sun would be. The hair is straight, black, coarse and abundant. The men usually wear it hanging below their ears, cut straight around, with a forehead bang reaching nearly to the eyebrows. The women wear it braided and looped up on the sides of the head.

What constitutes beauty is of course largely a question of individual taste. My own judgment of the Eskimos is that they are very ugly, although I have seen young women among them whom I thought actually handsome. This was when they first arrived at the Post with dogs and komatik and they were dressed in their native costume of deerskin trousers and Koolutuk, their cheeks red and glowing with the exercise of travel and the keen, frosty atmosphere. A half hour later I have seen the same women when stringy, dirty skirts had replaced the neat- fitting trousers, and Dr. Grenfell's description of them when thus clad invariably came to my mind: "A bedraggled kind of mop, soaked in oil and filth." This tendency to ape civilization by wearing civilized garments, is happily confined to their brief sojourns at the Post. When they are away at their camps and igloos their own costume is almost exclusively worn, and is the best possible costume for the climate and the country. The adikey, or koolutuk, of the women, has a long flap or tail, reaching nearly to the heels, and a sort of apron in front. The hood is so commodious in size that a baby can be tucked away into it, and that is the way the small children are carried. The men wear cloth trousers except in the very cold weather, when they don their deer or seal skins. Their adikey or koolutuk reaches half way to their knees, and is cut square around. The hood of course, in their case, is only large enough to cover the head. It might be of interest to explain that if this garment is made of cloth it is an adikey; if of deerskin, a koolutuk, and if made of sealskin, a netsek--all cut alike. If they wear two cloth garments at the same time, as is usually the case, the inner one only is an adikey, the outer one a silapak.

Their language is the same from Greenland to Alaska. Of course different localities have different dialects, but this is the natural result of a different environment. Missionary Bohlman, whom I met at Hebron, told me that before coming to Labrador

154

he was attached to a Greenland mission. When he came to Ms new field he found the language so similar to that in Greenland that he had very little difficulty in making himself understood. When Missionary Stecker a few years ago went from Labrador to Alaska he was able to converse with the Alaskan Eskimos. It is held by some authorities that Greenland was peopled by Labrador Eskimos who crossed Hudson Strait to Baffin Land, and thence made their way to Greenland, having originally crossed from Siberia into Alaska, thence eastward, skirting Hudson Bay. This is entirely feasible. I heard of one umiak (skin boat) only a few years ago having crossed to Cape Chidley from Baffin Land. Even in Labrador there are many different dialects. The "Northerners," the people inhabiting the northwest arm of the peninsula, have many words that the Koksoagmiut do not understand. The intonation of the Ungava Eskimos, particularly the women, is like a plaint. At Okak they sing their words. Each settlement on the Atlantic coast has its own dialect. It is a difficult language to learn. Words are compounded until they reach a great and almost unpronounceable length.* Naturally the coming of the trader has introduced many new words, as tobaccomik, teamik, etc., "mik" being the accusative ending. The Eskimo in his language cannot count beyond ten. If he wishes to express twelve, for instance, he will say, "as many fingers as a man has and two more." To express one hundred he would say, "five times as many fingers and toes as a man has," and so on. It is not a written language, but the Moravians have adapted the English alphabet to it and are teaching the Eskimos to read and write. Mr. Stewart in his work has adapted the Cree syllabic characters to the Eskimo, and he is teaching the Ungava people to write by this method, which is largely phonetic. Both the Moravians and Mr. Stewart are instructing them in the mystery of counting in German.

*The following will illustrate this; it is part of a sentence quoted from a Moravian missionary pamphlet:

"Taimailinganiarpok, illagget Labradormiut namgminek akkilejungnalerkartinaget pijariakartamingnik tamainik, sakkertitsijungnalerkartinagillo ajokertnijunik."

** The Eskimo numerals are as follows: 1, attansek; 2, magguk; 3, pingasut; 4, sittamat; 5, tellimat; 6, pingasoyortut;

7, aggartut; 8, sittamauyortut; 9, sittamartut; 10, tellimauyortut.

Cleanliness is not one of the Eskimos' virtues, and they are frequently infested with vermin, which are wont to transfer their allegiance to visitors, as we learned in due course, to our discomfiture. For many months of the year the only water they have is obtained by melting snow or ice. In sections where there is no wood for fuel this must be done over stone lamps in which seal oil is burned, and it is so slow a process that the water thus procured is held too precious to be wasted in cleansing body or clothing. One of the missionaries remarked that "the children must be very clean little creatures, for the parents never find it necessary to wash them."

They treat the children with the greatest kindness and consideration-- not only their own, but all children, generally. I did not once see an Eskimo punish a child, nor hear a harsh word spoken to one, and they are the most obedient youngsters in the world. A missionary on the Atlantic coast told me that once when he punished his child an Eskimo standing near remarked: "You don't love you child or you wouldn't punish it." And this is the sentiment they hold.

Love is not essential to a happy marriage among the Eskimos. When a man wants a woman he takes her. In fact they believe that an unwilling bride makes a good wife. Potokomik's wife was most unwilling, and he took her, dragging her by the tail of her adikey from her father's igloo across the river on the ice to his own, and they have "lived happily ever after," which seems to prove the correctness of the Eskimo theory as to unwilling brides. Of course if Potokomik's wife had not liked him after a fair trial, she could have left him, or if she had not come up to his expectations he could have sent her back home and tried another. It is all quite simple, for there is no marriage ceremony and resort to South Dakota courts for divorce is unnecessary. If a man wants two wives, why he has them, if there are women enough. That, too, is a very agreeable arrangement, for when he is away hunting the women keep each other company. Small families are the rule, and I did not hear of a case where twins had ever been born to the Eskimos.

Dancing and football are among their chief pastimes. The

men enter into the dance with zest, but the women as though they were performing some awful penance. Both sexes play football. They have learned the use of cards and are reckless gamblers, sometimes staking even the garments on their backs in play.

The Eskimo is a close bargainer, and after he has agreed to do you a service for a consideration will as likely as not change his mind at the last moment and leave you in the lurch. At the same time he is in many respects a child.

The dwellings are of three kinds: The tupek--skin tent; igloowiuk-- snow house; and permanent igloo, built of driftwood, stones and turf-- the larger ones are igloosoaks.

Flesh and fish, as is the case with the Indians, form the principal food, but while the Indians cook everything the Eskimos as often eat their meat and fish raw, and are not too particular as to its age or state of decay. They are very fond of venison and seal meat, and for variety's sake welcome dog meat. A few years ago a disease carried off several of the dogs at Fort Chimo and every carcass was eaten. One old fellow, in fact, as Mathewson related to me, ate nothing else during that time, and when the epidemic was over bemoaned the fact that no more dog meat could be had.

On the Atlantic coast where the snow houses are not used and the Eskimos live more generally during the winter in the close, vile igloos, there is more or less tubercular trouble. Even farther south, where the natives have learned cleanliness, and live in comfortable log cabins that are fairly well aired, this is the prevailing disease. After leaving Ramah, the farther south you go the more general is the adoption of civilized customs, food and habits of life, and with the increase of civilization so also comes an increased death rate amongst the Eskimos. Formerly there was a considerable number of these people on the Straits of Belle Isle. Now there is not one there. South of Hamilton Inlet but two full-blood Eskimos remain. Below Ramah the deaths exceed the births, and at one settlement alone there are fifty less people to-day than three years ago.

Civilization is responsible for this. At the present time there remains on the Atlantic coast, between the Straits of Belle Isle and Cape Chidley, but eleven hundred and twenty-seven full-blood Eskimos. Five years hence there will not be a thousand.

In Ungava district, where they have as yet accepted practically nothing of civilization, the births exceed the deaths, and I did not learn of a single well authenticated case of tuberculosis while I was there. There were a few cases of rheumatism. Death comes early, however, owing to the life of constant hardship and exposure. Usually they do not exceed sixty or sixty-five years of age, though I saw one man that had rounded his three score years and ten.

Formerly they encased their dead in skins and lay them out upon the rocks with the clothing and things they had used in life. Now rough wooden boxes are provided by the traders. The dogs in time break the coffins open and pick the bones, which lie uncared for, to be bleached by the frosts of winter and suns of summer. Mr. Stewart has collected and buried many of these bones, and is endeavoring now to have all bodies buried.

Of all the missionaries that I met in this bleak northern land, devoted as every one of them is to his life work, none was more devoted and none was doing a more self-sacrificing work than the Rev. Samuel Milliken Stewart of Fort Chimo. His novitiate as a missionary was begun in one of the little out-port fishing villages of Newfoundland. Finally he was transferred to that fearfully barren stretch among the heathen Eskimos north of Nachvak. Here he and his Eskimo servant gathered together such loose driftwood as they could find, and with this and stones and turf erected a single-roomed igloo. It was a small affair, not over ten by twelve or fourteen feet in size, and an imaginary line separated the missionary's quarters from his servant's. On his knees, in an old resting place for the dead, with the bleaching bones of heathen Eskimos strewn over the rocks about him, he consecrated his life efforts to the conversion of this people to Christianity. Then he went to work to accomplish this purpose in a businesslike way. He set himself the infinite task of mastering the difficult language. He lived their life with them, visiting and sleeping with them in their filthy igloos--so filthy and so filled with stench from the putrid meat and fish scraps that they permit to lie about and decay that frequently at first, until he became accustomed to it, he was forced to seek the open air and relieve the resulting nausea. But Stewart is a man of iron will, and he never wavered. He studied his people, administered medicines to the sick, and taught the doctrines of Christianity--Love, Faith and Charity--at every opportunity. That first winter was a trying one. All his little stock of fuel was exhausted early. The few articles of furniture that be had brought with him he burned to help keep out the frost demon, and before spring suffered greatly with the cold. The winter before our arrival he transferred his efforts to the Fort Chimo district, where his field would be larger and he could reach a greater number of the heathens. During the journey to Fort Chimo, which was across the upper peninsula, with dogs, he was lost in storms that prevailed at the time, his provisions were exhausted, and one dog had been killed to feed the others, before he finally met Eskimos who guided him in safety to George River. At Fort Chimo the Hudson's Bay Company set aside two small buildings to his use, one for a chapel, the other a little cabin in which he lives. Here we found him one day with a pot of high-smelling seal meat cooking for his dogs and a pan of dough cakes frying for himself. With Stewart in this cabin I spent many delightful hours. His constant flow of well-told stories, flavored with native Irish wit, was a sure panacea for despondency. I believe Stewart, with his sunny temperament, is really enjoying his life amongst the heathen, and he has made an obvious impression upon them, for every one of them turns out to his chapel meetings, where the services are conducted in Eskimo, and takes part with a will.

The Eskimo religion, like that of the Indian, is one of fear. Numerous are the spirits that people the land and depths of the sea, but the chief of them all is Torngak, the spirit of Death, who from his cavern dwelling in the heights of the mighty Torngaeks (the mountains north of the George River toward Cape Chidley) watches them always and rules their fortunes with an iron hand, dealing out misfortune, or withholding it, at his will. It is only through the medium of the Angakok, or conjurer, that the people can learn what to do to keep Torngak and the lesser spirits of evil, with their varying moods, in good humor. Stewart has led some of the Eskimos to at least outwardly renounce their heathenism and profess Christianity. In a few instances I believe they are sincere. If he remains upon the field, as I know he wishes to do, he will have them all professing Christianity within the next few years, for they like him. But he has no more regard for danger, when he believes duty calls him, than Dr. Grenfell has, and it is predicted on the coast that someday Dr. Grenfell will take one chance too many with the elements.

Of course, coming among the Eskimos as we did in winter, we did not see them using their kayaks or their umiaks,* but our experience with dogs and komatik was pretty complete. These dogs are big wolfish creatures, which resemble wolves so closely in fact that when the dogs and wolves are together the one can scarcely be told from the other. It sometimes happens that a stray wolf will hobnob with the dogs, and litters of half wolf, half dog have been born at the posts.

* A large open boat with wooden frame and sealskin covering. The women row the umiaks while the men sit idle. It is beneath the dignity of the latter to handle the oars when women are present to do it.

There are no better Eskimo dogs to be found anywhere in the far north than the husky dogs of Ungava. Wonderful tales are told of long distances covered by them in a single day, the record trip of which I heard being one hundred and twelve miles. But this was in the spring, when the days were long and the snow hard and firm. The farthest I ever traveled myself in a single day with dogs and komatik was sixty miles. When the snow is loose and the days are short, twenty to thirty miles constitute a day's work.

From five to twelve dogs are usually driven in one team, though sometimes a man is seen plodding along with a two-dog team, and occasionally as many as sixteen or eighteen are harnessed to a komatik, but these very large teams are unwieldy.

The komatiks in the Ungava district vary from ten to eighteen feet in length. The runners are about two and one-half inches thick at the bottom, tapering slightly toward the top to reduce friction where they sink into the snow. They are usually placed sixteen inches apart, and crossbars extending about an inch over the outer runner on either side are lashed across the runners by means of thongs of sealskin or heavy twine, which is passed through holes bored into the crossbars and the runners. The use of lashings instead of nails or screws permits the komatik to yield readily in passing over rough places, where metal fastenings would be pulled out, or be snapped off by the frost. On either side of each end of the overlapping ends of the crossbars notches are cut, around which sealskin thongs are passed in lashing on the load. The bottoms of the komatik runners are "mudded." During the summer the Eskimos store up turf for this purpose, testing bits of it by chewing it to be sure that it contains no grit. When the cold weather comes the turf is mixed with warm water until it reaches the consistency of mud. Then with the hands it is molded over the bottom of the runners. The mud quickly freezes, after which it is carefully planed smooth and round. Then it is iced by applying warm water with a bit of hairy deerskin. These mudded runners slip very smoothly over the soft snow, but are liable to chip off on rough ice or when they strike rocks, as frequently happens, for the frozen mud is as brittle as glass. On the Atlantic coast from Nachvak south, mud is never used, and there the komatiks are wider and shorter with runners of not much more than half the thickness, and as you go south the komatiks continue to grow wider and shorter. In the south, too, hoop iron or whalebone is used for runner shoeing.

A sealskin thong called a bridle, of a varying length of from twenty to forty feet, is attached to the front of the komatik, and to the end of this the dogs' traces are fastened. Each dog has an individual trace which may be from eight to thirty feet in length, depending upon the size of the team, so arranged that not more than two dogs are abreast, the "leader" having, of course, the longest trace of the pack. This long bridle and the long traces are made necessary by the rough country. They permit the animals to swerve well to one side clear of the komatik when coasting down a hillside. In the length of bridle and trace there is also a wide variation in different sections, those used in the south being very much shorter than those in the north. The dog harness is made usually of polar bear or sealskin. There are no reins. The driver controls his team by shouting directions, and with a walrus hide whip, which is from twenty-five to thirty-five feet in length. An expert with this whip, running after the dogs, can hit any dog he chooses at will, and sometimes he is cruel to excess.

To start his team the driver calls "oo-isht," (in the south this becomes "hoo-eet") to turn to the right "ouk," to the left "ra-der, ra-der" and to stop "aw-aw." The leader responds to the shouted directions and the pack follow.

The Ungava Eskimo never upon any account travels with komatik and dogs without a snow knife. With this implement he can in a little while make himself a comfortable snow igloo, where he may spend the night or wait for a storm to pass.

In winter it is practically impossible to buy a dog in Ungava. The people have only enough for their own use, and will not part with them, and if they have plenty to eat it is difficult to employ them for any purpose. This I discovered very promptly when I endeavored to induce some of them to take us a stage on our journey homeward.

Chapter 20: The Sledge Journey Begun

Tighter and tighter grew the grip of winter. Rarely the temperature rose above twenty-five degrees below zero, even at midday, and oftener it crept well down into the thirties. The air was filled with rime, which clung to everything, and the sun, only venturing now a little way above the southern horizon, shone cold and cheerless, weakly penetrating the ever-present frost veil. The tide, still defying the shackles of the mighty power that had bound all the rest of the world, surged up and down, piling ponderous ice cakes in mountainous heaps along the river banks. Occasionally an Eskimo or two would suddenly appear out of the snow fields, remain for a day perhaps, and then as suddenly disappear into the bleak wastes whence he had come.

Slowly the days dragged along. We occupied the short hours of light in reading old newspapers and magazines, or walking out over the hills, and in the evenings called upon the Post officers or entertained them in our cabin, where Mathewson often came to smoke his after-supper pipe and relate to us stories of his forty-odd years' service as a fur trader in the northern wilderness.

One bitter cold morning, long before the first light of day began to filter through the rimy atmosphere, we heard the crunch of feet pass our door, and a komatik slipped by. It was Dr. Milne, away to George River and the coast on his tour of Post inspection, and our little group of white men was one less in number.

We envied him his early leaving. We could not ourselves start for home until after New Year's, for there were no dogs to be had for love or money until the Eskimos came in from their hunting camps to spend the holidays. Everything, however, was made ready for that longed-for time. Through the kindness of The'venet, who put his Post folk to work for us, the deerskins I had brought from Whale River were dressed and made up into sleeping bags and skin clothing, and other necessities were made ready for the long dog journey out.

Christmas eve came finally, and with it komatik loads of Eskimos, who roused the place from its repose into comparative wakefulness. The newcomers called upon us in twos or threes, never troubling to knock before they entered our cabin, looked us and our things over with much interest, a proceeding which occupied usually a full half hour, then went away, sometimes to bring back newly arriving friends, to introduce them. A multitude of dogs skulked around by day and made night hideous with howling and fighting, and it was hardly safe to walk abroad without a stick, of which they have a wholesome fear, as, like their progenitors, the wolves, they are great cowards and will rarely attack a man when he has any visible means of defense at hand.

Christmas afternoon was given over to shooting matches, and the evening to dancing. We spent the day with The'venet. Mathewson was not in position to entertain, as the Indian woman that presided in his kitchen partook so freely of liquor of her own manufacture that she became hilariously drunk early in the morning, and for the peace of the household and safety of the dishes, which she playfully shied at whoever came within reach, she was ejected, and Mathewson prepared his own meals. At The'venet's, however, everything went smoothly, and the sumptuous meal of baked whitefish, venison, with canned vegetables, plum pudding, cheese and coffee--delicacies held in reserve for the occasion--made us forget the bleak wilderness and ice-bound land in which we were.

It seemed for a time even now as though we should not be able to secure dogs and drivers. No one knew the way to Ramah, and on no account would one of these Eskimos undertake even a part of the journey without permission from the Hudson's Bay Company. As a last resort The'venet promised me his dogs and driver to take us at least as far as George River, but finally Emuk arrived and an arrangement was made with him to carry us from Whale River to George River, and two other Eskimos agreed to go with us to Whale River. The great problem that confronted me now was how to get over the one hundred and sixty miles of barrens from George River to Ramah, and it was necessary to arrange for this before leaving Fort Chimo, as dogs to the eastward were even scarcer than here. Mathewson finally solved it for me with his promise to instruct Ford at George River to put his team and drivers at my disposal. Thus, after much bickering, our relays were arranged as far as the Moravian mission station at Ramah, and I trusted in Providence and the coast Eskimos to see us on from there. The third of January was fixed as the day of our departure.

Our going in winter was an event. It gave the Post folk an opportunity to send out a winter mail, which I volunteered to carry to Quebec.

Straggling bands of Indians, hauling fur-laden toboggans, began to arrive during the week, and the bartering in the stores was brisk, and to me exceedingly interesting. Money at Fort Chimo is unknown. Values are reckoned in "skins"--that is, a "skin" is the unit of value. There is no token of exchange to represent this unit, however, and if a hunter brings in more pelts than sufficient to pay for his purchases, the trader simply gives him credit on his books for the balance due, to be drawn upon at some future time. As a matter of fact, the hunter is almost invariably in debt to the store. A "skin" will buy a pint of molasses, a quarter pound of tea or a quarter pound of black stick tobacco. A white arctic fox pelt is valued at seven skins, a blue fox pelt at twelve, and a black or silver fox at eighty to ninety skins. South of Hamilton Inlet, where competition is keen with the fur traders, they pay in cash six dollars for white, eight dollars for blue (which, by the way, are very scarce there) and not infrequently as high as three hundred and fifty dollars or even more for black and silver fox pelts. The cost of maintaining posts at Fort Chimo, however, is somewhat greater than at these southern points.

Here at Ungava the Eskimos' hunt is confined almost wholly to foxes, polar bears, an occasional wolf and wolverine, and, of course, during the season, seals, walrus, and white whales. An average hunter will trap from sixty to seventy foxes in a season, though one or two exceptional ones I knew have captured as many as two hundred. The Indians, who penetrate far into the interior, bring out marten, mink and otter principally, with a few foxes, an occasional beaver, black bear, lynx and some wolf and wolverine skins. There is a story of a very large and ferocious brown bear that tradition says inhabits the barrens to the eastward toward George River. Mr. Peter McKenzie told me that many years ago, when he was stationed at Fort Chimo, the Indians brought him one of the skins of this animal, and Ford at George River said that, some twenty years since, he saw a piece of one of the skins. Both agreed that the hair was very long, light brown in color, silver tipped and of a decidedly different species from either the polar or black bear. This is the only definite information as to it that I was able to gather. The Indians speak of it with dread, and insist that it is still to be found, though none of them can say positively that he has seen one in a decade. I am inclined to believe that the brown bear, so far as Labrador is concerned, has been exterminated.

New Year's is the great day at Fort Chimo. All morning there were shooting matches and foot races, and in the afternoon football games in progress, in which the Eskimo men and women alike joined. The Indians, who were recovering from an all-night drunk on their vile beer, and a revel in the "Queen's" cabin, condescended to take part in the shooting matches, but held majestically aloof from the other games. Some of them came into the French store in the evening to squat around the room and watch the dancing while they puffed in silence on their pipes and drank tea when it was passed. That was their only show of interest in the festivities. Early on the morning of the second they all disappeared. But these were only a fragment of those that visit the Post in summer. It is then that they have their powwow.

At last the day of our departure arrived, with a dull leaden sky and that penetrating cold that eats to one's very marrow. The'venet and Belfleur came early and brought us a box of cigars to ease the tedium of the long evenings in the snow houses. All the little colony of white men were on hand to see us off, and I believe were genuinely sorry to have us go, for we had become a part of the little coterie and our coming had made a break in the lives of these lonely exiles. Men brought together under such conditions become very much attached to each other in a short time. "It's going to be lonesome now," said Stewart. "I'm sorry you have to leave us. May God speed you on your way, and carry you through your long journey in safety."

Finally our baggage was lashed on the komatik; the dogs, leaping and straining at their traces, howled their eagerness to be gone; we shook hands warmly with everybody, even the Eskimos, who came forward wondering at what seemed to them our stupendous undertaking, the komatik was "broken" loose, and we were away at a gallop.

Traveling was good, and the nine dogs made such excellent time that we had to ride in level places or we could not have kept pace with them. When there was a hill to climb we pushed on the komatik or hauled with the dogs on the long bridle to help them along. When we had a descent to make, the drag--a hoop of walrus hide--was thrown over the front end of one of the komatik runners at the top, and if the place was steep the Eskimos, one on either side of the komatik, would cling on with their arms and brace their feet into the snow ahead, doing their utmost to hold back and reduce the momentum of the heavy sledge. To the uninitiated they would appear to be in imminent danger of having their legs broken, for the speed down some of the grades when the crust was hard and icy was terrific. When descending the gentler slopes we all rode, depending upon the drag alone to keep our speed within reason. This coasting downhill was always an exciting experience, and where the going was rough it was not easy to keep a seat on the narrow komatik. Occasionally the komatik would turn over. When we saw this was likely to happen we discreetly dropped off, a feat that demanded agility and practice to be performed successfully and gracefully.

It was a relief beyond measure to feel that we were at length, after seven long months, actually headed toward home and civilization. Words cannot express the feeling of exhilaration that comes to one at such a time.

We did not have to go so far up Whale River to find a crossing as on our trip to Fort Chimo, and reached the eastern side before dark. Sometimes the ice hills are piled so high here by the tide that it takes a day or even two to cut a komatik path through them and cross the river, but fortunately we had very little cutting to do. Not long after dark we coasted down the hill above the Post, and the cheerful lights of Edmunds' cabin were at hand.

Here we had to wait two days for Emuk, and in the interim Mrs. Edmunds and Mary went carefully over our clothes, sewed sealskin legs to deerskin moccasins, made more duffel socks, and with kind solicitation put all our things into the best of shape and gave us extra moccasins and mittens. "It is well to have plenty of everything before you start," said Mrs. Edmunds, "for if the huskies are hunting deer the women will do no sewing on sealskin, and if they're hunting seals they'll not touch a needle to your deerskins, though you are freezing."

"Why is that?" I asked.

"Oh, some of their heathen beliefs," she answered. "They think it would bring bad luck to the hunters. They believe all kinds of foolishness."

Emuk had never been so far away as George River, and Sam Ford was to be our pilot to that point, and to return with Emuk. The Eskimos do not consider it safe for a man to travel alone with dogs, and they never do it when there is the least probability that they will have to remain out overnight. Two men are always required to build a snow igloo, which is one reason for this. It was therefore necessary for me at each point, when employing the Eskimo driver for a new stage of our journey, also to engage a companion for him, that he might have company when returning home.

Our coming to Whale River two months before had made a welcome innovation in the even tenor of the cheerless, lonely existence of our good friends at the Post--an event in their confined life, and they were really sorry to part from us.

"It will be a long time before any one comes to see us again-- a long time," said Mrs. Edmunds, sadly adding: "I suppose no one will ever come again."

When we said our farewells the women cried. In their Godspeed the note of friendship rang true and honest and sincere. These people had proved themselves in a hundred ways. In civilization, where the selfish instinct governs so generally, there are too many Judases. On the frontier, in spite of the rough exterior of the people, you find real men and women. That is one reason why I like the North so well.

We left Whale River on Saturday, the sixth of January, with

one hundred and twenty miles of barrens to cross before reaching George River Post, the nearest human habitation to the eastward. Our fresh team of nine dogs was in splendid trim and worked well, but a three or four inch covering of light snow upon the harder under crust made the going hard and wearisome for the animals. The frost flakes that filled the air covered everything. Clinging to the eyelashes and faces of the men it gave them a ghostly appearance, our skin clothing was white with it, long icicles weighted our beards, and the sharp atmosphere made it necessary to grasp one's nose frequently to make certain that the member was not freezing.

When we stopped for the night our snow house which Emuk and Sam soon had ready seemed really cheerful. Our halt was made purposely near a cluster of small spruce where enough firewood was found to cook our supper of boiled venison, hard-tack and tea, water being procured by melting ice. Spruce boughs were scattered upon the igloo floor and deerskins spread over these.

After everything was made snug, and whatever the dogs might eat or destroy put safely out of their reach, the animals were unharnessed and fed the one meal that was allowed them each day after their work was done. Feeding the dogs was always an interesting function. While one man cut the frozen food into chunks, the rest of us armed with cudgels beat back the animals. When the word was given we stepped to one side to avoid the onrush as they came upon the food, which was bolted with little or no chewing. They will eat anything that is fed them--seal meat, deer's meat, fish, or even old hides. There was always a fight or two to settle after the feeding and then the dogs made holes for themselves in the snow and lay down for the drift to cover them.

The dogs fed, we crawled with our hot supper into the igloo, put a block of snow against the entrance and stopped the chinks around it with loose snow. Then the kettle covers were lifted and the place was filled at once with steam so thick that one could hardly see his elbow neighbor. By the time the meal was eaten the temperature had risen to such a point that the place was quite warm and comfortable--so warm that the snow in the top of the igloo was soft enough to pack but not quite soft enough to drip water. Then we smoked some of The'venet's cigars and blessed him for his thoughtfulness in providing them.

Usually our snow igloos allowed each man from eighteen to twenty inches space in which to lie down, and just room enough to stretch his legs well. With our sleeping bags they were entirely comfortable, no matter what the weather outside. The snow is porous enough to admit of air circulation, but even a gale of wind without would not affect the temperature within. It is claimed by the natives that when the wind blows, a snow house is warmer than in a period of still cold. I could see no difference. A new snow igloo is, however, more comfortable than one that has been used, for newly cut snow blocks are more porous. In one that has been used there is always a crust of ice on the interior which prevents a proper circulation of air.

On the second day we passed the shack where Easton and I had held our five-day fast, and shortly after came out upon the plains--a wide stretch of flat, treeless country where no hills rise as guiding landmarks for the voyageur. This was beyond the zone of Emuk's wanderings, and Sam went several miles astray in his calculations, which, in view of the character of the country, was not to be wondered at, piloting as he did without a compass. However, we were soon set right and passed again into the rolling barrens, with ever higher hills with each eastern mile we traveled.

At two o'clock on the afternoon of Tuesday, January ninth, we dropped over the bank upon the ice of George River just above the Post, and at three o'clock were under Mr. Ford's hospitable roof again.

Here we had to encounter another vexatious delay of a week. Ford's dogs had been working hard and were in no condition to travel and not an Eskimo team was there within reach of the Post that could be had. There was nothing to do but wait for Ford's team to rest and get into condition before taking them upon the trying journey across the barren grounds that lay between us and the Atlantic.

Chapter 21: Crossing the Barrens

On Tuesday morning, January sixteenth, we swung out upon the river ice with a powerful team of twelve dogs. Will Ford and an Eskimo named Etuksoak, called by the Post folk "Peter," for short, were our drivers.

The dogs began the day with a misunderstanding amongst themselves, and stopped to fight it out. When they were finally beaten into docility one of them, apparently the outcast of the pack, was limping on three legs and leaving a trail of blood behind him. Every team has its bully, and sometimes its outcast. The bully is master of them all. He fights his way to his position of supremacy, and holds it by punishing upon the slightest provocation, real or fancied, any encroachment upon his autocratic prerogatives. Likewise he disciplines the pack when he thinks they need it or when he feels like it, and he is always the ringleader in mischief. When there is an outcast he is a doomed dog. The others harass and fight him at every opportunity. They are pitiless. They do not associate with him, and sooner or later a morning will come when they are noticed licking their chops contentedly, as dogs do when they have had a good meal-- and after that no more is seen of the outcast. The bully is not always, or, in fact, often the leader in harness. The dog that the driver finds most intelligent in following a trail and in answering his commands is chosen for this important position, regardless of his fighting prowess.

This morning as we started the weather was perfect--thirty-odd degrees below zero and a bright sun that made the hoar frost sparkle like flakes of silver. For ten miles our course lay down the river to a point just below the "Narrows." Then we left the ice and hit the overland trail in an almost due northerly direction. It was a rough country and there was much pulling and hauling and pushing to be done crossing the hills. Before noon the wind began to rise, and by the time we stopped to prepare our snow igloo for the night a northwest gale had developed and the air was filled with drifting snow.

Early in the afternoon I began to have cramps in the calves of my legs, and finally it seemed to me that the muscles were tied into knots. Sharp, intense pains in the groin made it torture to lift in feet above the level of the snow, and I was never more thankful for rest in my life than when that day's work was finished. Easton confessed to me that he had an attack similar to my own. This was the result of our inactivity at Fort Chimo. We were suffering with what among the Canadian voyageurs is known as mal de roquette. There was nothing to do but endure it without complaint, for there is no relief until in time it gradually passes away of its own accord.

This first night from George River was spent upon the shores of a lake which, hidden by drifted snow, appeared to be about two miles wide and seven or eight miles long. It lay amongst low, barren hills, where a few small bunches of gnarled black spruce relieved the otherwise unbroken field of white.

The following morning it was snowing and drifting, and as the day grew the storm increased. An hour's traveling carried us to the Koroksoak River--River of the Great Gulch--which flows from the northeast, following the lower Torngaek mountains and emptying into Ungava Bay near the mouth of the George. The Koroksoak is apparently a shallow stream, with a width of from fifty to two hundred yards. Its bed forms the chief part of the komatik route to Nachvak, and therefore our route. For several miles the banks are low and sandy, but farther up the sand disappears and the hills crowd close upon the river. The gales that sweep down the valley with every storm had blown away the snow and drifted the bank sand in a layer over the river ice. This made the going exceedingly hard and ground the mud from the komatik runners.

The snowstorm, directly in our teeth, increased in force with every mile we traveled, and with the continued cramps and pains in my legs it seemed to me that the misery of it all was about as refined and complete as it could be. It may be imagined, therefore, the relief I felt when at noon Will and Peter stopped the komatik with the announcement that we must camp, as further progress could not be made against the blinding snow and head wind.

Advantage was taken of the daylight hours to mend the komatik mud. This was done by mixing caribou moss with water, applying the mixture to the mud where most needed, and permitting it to freeze, which it did instantly. Then the surface was planed smooth with a little jack plane carried for the purpose.

That night the storm blew itself out, and before daylight, after a breakfast of coffee and hard-tack, we were off. The half day's rest had done wonders for me, and the pains in my legs were not nearly so severe as on the previous day.

January and February see the lowest temperatures of the Labrador winter. Now the cold was bitter, rasping--so intensely cold was the atmosphere that it was almost stifling as it entered the lungs. The vapor from our nostrils froze in masses of ice upon our beards. The dogs, straining in the harness, were white with hoar frost, and our deerskin clothing was also thickly coated with it. For long weeks these were to be the prevailing conditions in our homeward march.

Dark and ominous were the spruce-lined river banks on either side that morning as we toiled onward, and grim and repellent indeed were the rocky hills outlined against the sky beyond. Everything seemed frozen stiff and dead except ourselves. No sound broke the absolute silence save the crunch, crunch, crunch of our feet, the squeak of the komatik runners complaining as they slid reluctantly over the snow, and the "oo-isht-oo-isht, oksuit, oksuit" of the drivers, constantly urging the dogs to greater effort. Shimmering frost flakes, suspended in the air like a veil of thinnest gauze, half hid the sun when very timidly he raised his head above the southeastern horizon, as though afraid to venture into the domain of the indomitable ice king who had wrested the world from his last summer's power and ruled it now so absolutely.

With every mile the spruce on the river banks became thinner and thinner, and the hills grew higher and higher, until finally there was scarcely a stick to be seen and the lower eminences had given way to lofty mountains which raised their jagged, irregular peaks from two to four thousand feet in solemn and majestic grandeur above our heads. The gray basaltic rocks at their base shut in the tortuous river bed, and we knew now why the Koroksoak was called the "River of the Great Gulch." These were the mighty Torngaeks, which farther north attain an altitude above the sea of full seven thousand feet. We passed the place where Torngak dwells in his mountain cavern and sends forth his decrees to the spirits of Storm and Starvation and Death to do destruction, or restrains them, at his will.

In the forenoon of the third day after leaving George River we stopped to lash a few sticks on top of our komatik load. "No more wood," said Will. "This'll have to see us through to Nachvak." That afternoon we turned out of the Koroksoak River into a pass leading to the northward, and that night's igloo was at the headwaters of a stream that they said ran into Nachvak Bay.

The upper part of this new gulch was strewn with boulders, and much hard work and ingenuity were necessary the following morning to get the komatik through them at all. Farther down the stream widened. Here the wind had swept the snow clear of the ice, and it was as smooth as a piece of glass, broken only by an occasional boulder sticking above the surface. A heavy wind blew in our backs and carried the komatik before it at a terrific pace, with the dogs racing to keep out of the way. Sometimes we were carried sidewise, sometimes stern first, but seldom right end foremost. Lively work was necessary to prevent being wrecked upon the rocks, and occasionally we did turn over, when a boulder was struck side on.

There were several steep down grades. Before descending one of the first of these a line was attached to the rear end of the komatik and Will asked Easton to hang on to it and hold back, to keep the komatik straight. There was no foothold for him, however, on the smooth surface of the ice, and Easton found that he could not hold back as directed. The momentum was considerable, and he was afraid to let go for fear of losing his balance on the slippery ice, and so, wild-eyed and erect, he slid along, clinging for dear life to the line. Pretty soon he managed to attain a sitting posture, and with his legs spread before him, but still holding desperately on, he skimmed along after the komatik. The next and last evolution was a "belly-gutter" position. This became too strenuous for him, however, and the line was jerked out of his hands. I was afraid he might have been injured on a rock, but my anxiety was soon relieved when I saw him running along the shore to overtake the komatik where it had been stopped to wait for him below.

This gulch was exceedingly narrow, with mountains, lofty, rugged and grand rising directly from the stream's bank, some of them attaining an altitude of five thousand feet or more. At one point they squeezed the brook through a pass only ten feet in width, with perpendicular walls towering high above our heads on either side. This place is known to the Hudson's Bay Company people as "The Porch."

In the afternoon Peter caught his foot in a crevice, and the komatik jammed him with such force that he narrowly escaped a broken leg and was crippled for the rest of the journey. Early in the afternoon we were on salt water ice, and at two o'clock sighted Nachvak Post of the Hudson's Bay Company, and at half past four were hospitably welcomed by Mrs. Ford, the wife of George Ford, the agent.

This was Saturday, January twentieth. Since the previous Tuesday morning we had had no fire to warm ourselves by and had been living chiefly on hard-tack, and the comfort and luxury of the Post sitting room, with the hot supper of arctic hare that came in due course, were appreciated. Mr. Ford had gone south with Dr. Milne to Davis Inlet Post and was not expected back for a week, but Mrs. Ford and her son Solomon Ford, who was in charge during his father's absence, did everything possible for our comfort.

The injury to Peter's leg made it out of the question for him to go on with us, and we therefore found it necessary to engage another team to carry us to Ramah, the first of the Moravian missionary stations on our route of travel, and this required a day's delay at Nachvak, as no Eskimos could be seen that night. The Fords offered us every assistance in securing drivers, and went to much trouble on our behalf. Solomon personally took it upon himself to find dogs and drivers for us, and through his kindness arrangements were made with two Eskimos, Taikrauk and Nikartok by name, who agreed to furnish a team of ten dogs and be on hand early on Monday morning. I considered myself fortunate in securing so large a team, for the seal hunt had been bad the previous fall and the Eskimos had therefore fallen short of dog food and had killed a good many of their dogs. I should not have been so ready with my self-congratulation had I seen the dogs that we were to have.

Nachvak is the most God-forsaken place for a trading post that I have ever seen. Wherever you look bare rocks and towering mountains stare you in the face; nowhere is there a tree or shrub of any kind to relieve the rock-bound desolation, and every bit of fuel has to be brought in during the summer by steamer. They have coal, but even the wood to kindle the coal is imported. The Eskimos necessarily use stone lamps in which seal oil is burned to heat their igloos. The Fords have lived here for a quarter of a century, but now the Company is abandoning the Post as unprofitable and they are to be transferred to some other quarter.

"God knows how lonely it is sometimes," Mrs. Ford said to me, "and how glad I'll be if we go where there's someone besides just greasy heathen Eskimos to see."

The Moravian mission at Killenek, a station three days' travel to the northward, on Cape Chidley, has deflected some of the former trade from Nachvak and the Ramah station more of it, until but twenty-seven Eskimos now remain at Nachvak.

Early on Monday morning not only our two Eskimos appeared, but the entire Eskimo population, even the women with babies in their hoods, to see us off. The ten-dog team that I had congratulated myself so proudly upon securing proved to be the most miserable aggregation of dogskin and bones I had ever seen, and in so horribly emaciated a condition that had there been any possible way of doing without them I should have declined to permit them to haul our komatik. However I had no choice, as no other dogs were to be had, and at six o'clock-- more than two hours before daybreak--we said farewell to good Mrs. Ford and her family and started forward with our caravan of followers.

We took what is known as the "outside" route, turning right out toward the mouth of the bay. By this route it is fully forty miles to Ramah. By a short cut overland, which is not so level, the distance is only about thirty miles, but our Eskimos chose the level course, as it is doubtful whether their excuses for dogs could have hauled the komatik over the hills on the short cut. An hour after our start we passed a collection of snow igloos, and all our following, after shaking hands and repeating, "Okusi," left us--all but one man, Korganuk by name, who decided to honor us with his society to Ramah; so we had three Eskimos instead of the more than sufficient two.

Though the traveling was fairly good the poor starved dogs crawled along so slowly that with a jog trot we easily kept in advance of them, and not even the extreme cruelty of the heathen drivers, who beat them sometimes unmercifully, could induce them to do better. I remonstrated with the human brutes on several occasions, but they pretended not to understand me, smiling blandly in return, and making unintelligible responses in Eskimo.

Before dawn the sky clouded, and by the time we reached the end of the bay and turned southward across the neck, toward noon, it began to snow heavily. This capped the climax of our troubles and I questioned whether our team would ever reach our destination with this added impediment of soft, new snow to plow through.

From the first the snow fell thick and fast. Then the wind rose, and with every moment grew in velocity. I soon realized that we were caught under the worst possible conditions in the throes of a Labrador winter storm--the kind of storm that has cost so many native travelers on that bleak coast their lives.

We were now on the ice again beyond the neck. Perpendicular, clifflike walls shut us off from retreat to the land and there was not a possibility of shelter anywhere. Previous snows had found no lodgment into banks, and an igloo could not be built. Our throats were parched with thirst, but there was no water to drink and nowhere a stick of wood with which to build a fire to melt snow. The dogs were lying down in harness and crying with distress, and the Eskimos had continually to kick them into renewed efforts. On we trudged, on and endlessly on. We were still far from our goal.

All of us, even the Eskimos, were utterly weary. Finally frequent stops were necessary to rest the poor toiling brutes, and we were glad to take advantage of each opportunity to throw ourselves at full length on the snow-covered ice for a moment's repose. Sometimes we would walk ahead of the komatik and lie down until it overtook us, frequently falling asleep in the brief interim. Now and again an Eskimo would look into my face and repeat, "Oksunae" (be strong), and I would encourage him in the same way.

Darkness fell thick and black. No signs of land were visible-- nothing but the whirling, driving, pitiless snow around us and the ice under our feet. Sometimes one of us would stumble on a hummock and fall, then rise again to resume the mechanical plodding. I wondered sometimes whether we were not going right out to sea and how long it would be before we should drop into open water and be swallowed up. My faculties were too benumbed to care much, and it was just a calculation in which I had no particular but only a passive interest.

The thirst of the snow fields is most agonizing, and can only be likened to the thirst of the desert. The snow around you is tantalizing, for to eat it does not quench the thirst in the slightest; it aggravates it. If I ever longed for water it was then.

Hour after hour passed and the night seemed interminable. But somehow we kept going, and the poor crying brutes kept going. All misery has its ending, however, and ours ended when I least looked for it. Un- expectedly the dogs' pitiful cries changed to gleeful howls and they visibly increased their efforts. Then Korganuk put his face close to mine and said: "Ramah! Ramah!" and quite suddenly we stopped before the big mission house at Ramah.

Chapter 22: On the Atlantic Ice

The dogs had stopped within a dozen feet of the building, but it was barely distinguishable through the thick clouds of smothering snow which the wind, risen to a terrific gale, swirled around us as it swept down in staggering gusts from the invisible hills above. A light filtered dimly through one of the frost-encrusted windows, and I tapped loudly upon the glass.

At first there was no response, but after repeated rappings someone moved within, and in a moment the door opened and a voice called to us, "Come, come out of the snow. It is a nasty night." Without further preliminaries we stepped into the shelter of the broad, comfortable hall. Holding a candle above his head, and peering at us through the dim light that it cast, was a short, stockily built, bearded man in his shirt sleeves and wearing hairy sealskin trousers and boots. To him I introduced myself and Easton, and he, in turn, told us that he was the Reverend Paul Schmidt, the missionary in charge of the station.

Mr. Schmidt's astonishment at our unexpected appearance at midnight and in such a storm was only equaled by his hospitable welcome. His broken English sounded sweet indeed, inviting us to throw off our snow-covered garments. He ushered us to a neat room on the floor above, struck a match to a stove already charged with kindling wood and coal, and in five minutes after our entrance we were listening to the music of a crackling fire and warming our chilled selves by its increasing heat.

Our host was most solicitous for our every comfort. He hurried in and out, and by the time we were thoroughly warmed told us supper was ready and asked us to his living room below, where Mrs. Schmidt had spread the table for a hot meal. Each mission house has a common kitchen and a common dining room, and besides having the use of these the separate families are each provided with a private living room and a sleeping room.

It is not pleasant to be routed out of bed in the middle of the night, but these good missionaries assured us that it was really a pleasure to them, and treated us like old friends whom they were overjoyed to see. "Well, well," said Mr. Schmidt, again and again, "it is very good for you to come. I am very glad that you came tonight, for now we shall have company, and you shall stay with us until the weather is fine again for traveling, and we will talk English together, which is a pleasure for me, for I have almost forgotten my English, with no one to talk it to."

It was after two o'clock when we went to bed, and I verily believe that Mr. Schmidt would have talked all night had it not been for our hard day's work and evident need of rest.

When we arose in the morning the storm was still blowing with unabated fury. We had breakfast with Mr. Schmidt in his private apartment and were later introduced to Mr. Karl Filsehke, the storekeeper, and his wife, who, like the Schmidts, were most hospitable and kind. At all of the Moravian missions, with the exception of Killinek "down to Chidley," and Makkovik, the farthest station "up south," there is, besides the missionary, who devotes himself more particularly to the spiritual needs of his people, a storekeeper who looks after their material welfare and assists in conducting the meetings.

In Labrador these missions are largely, though by no means wholly, self-supporting. Furs and blubber are taken from the Eskimos in exchange for goods, and the profits resulting from their sale in Europe are applied toward the expense of maintaining the stations. They own a small steamer, which brings the supplies from London every summer and takes away the year's accumulation of fur and oil. Since the first permanent establishment was erected at Nain, over one hundred and fifty years ago, they have followed this trade.

During the day I visited the store and blubber house, where Eskimo men and women were engaged in cutting seal blubber into small slices and pounding these with heavy wooden mallets. The pounded blubber is placed in zinc vats, and, when the summer comes, exposed in the vats to the sun's heat, which renders out a fine white oil. This oil is put into casks and shipped to the trade.

In the depth of winter seal hunting is impossible, and during that season the Eskimo families gather in huts, or igloosoaks, at the mission stations. There are sixty-nine of these people connected with the Ramah station and I visited them all with Mr. Schmidt. Their huts were heated with stone lamps and seal oil, for the country is bare of wood. The fuel for the mission house is brought from the South by the steamer.

The Eskimos at Ramah and at the stations south are all supposed to be Christians, but naturally they still retain many of the traditional beliefs and superstitions of their people. They will not live in a house where a death has occurred, believing that the spirit of the departed will haunt the place. If the building is worth it, they take it down and set it up again somewhere else.

Not long ago the wife of one of the Eskimos was taken seriously ill, and became delirious. Her husband and his neighbors, deciding that she was possessed of an evil spirit, tied her down and left her, until finally she died, uncared for and alone, from cold and lack of nourishment. This occurred at a distance from the station, and the missionaries did not learn of it until the woman was dead and beyond their aid. They are most kind in their ministrations to the sick and needy.

Once Dr. Grenfell visited Ramah and exhibited to the astonished Eskimos some stereopticon views--photographs that he had taken there in a previous year. It so happened that one of the pictures was that of an old woman who had died since the photograph was made, and when it appeared upon the screen terror struck the hearts of the simple-minded people. They believed it was her spirit returned to earth, and for a long time afterward imagined that they saw it floating about at night, visiting the woman's old haunts.

The daily routine of the mission station is most methodical. At seven o'clock in the morning a bell calls the servants to their duties; at nine o'clock it rings again, granting a half hour's rest; at a quarter to twelve a third ringing sends them to dinner; they return at one o'clock to work until dark. Every night at five o'clock the bell summons them to religious service in the chapel, where worship is conducted in Eskimo by either the missionary or the storekeeper. The women sit on one side, the men on the other, and are always in their seats before the last tone of the bell dies out. I used to enjoy these services exceedingly--watching the eager, expectant faces of the people as they heard the lesson taught, and their hearty singing of the hymns in Eskimo made the evening hour a most interesting one to me.

It is a busy life the missionary leads. From morning until night he is kept constantly at work, and in the night his rest is often broken by calls to minister to the sick. He is the father of his flock, and his people never hesitate to call for his help and advice; to him all their troubles and disagreements are referred for a wise adjustment.

I am free to say that previous to meeting them upon their field of labor I looked upon the work of these missionaries with indifference, if not disfavor, for I had been led to believe that they were accomplishing little or nothing. But now I have seen, and I know of what incalculable value the services are that they are rendering to the poor, benighted people of this coast.

They practically renounce the world and their home ties to spend their lives, until they are too old for further service or their health breaks down, in their Heaven-inspired calling, surrounded by people of a different race and language, in the most barren, God-cursed land in the world.

When their children reach the age of seven years they must send them to the church school at home to be educated. Very often parent and child never meet again. This is, as many of them told me, the greatest sacrifice they are called upon to make, but they realize that it is for the best good of the child and their work, and they do not murmur. What heroes and heroines these men and women are! One must admire and honor them.

There were some little ones here at Ramah who used to climb upon my knees and call me "Uncle," and kiss me good morning and good night, and I learned to love them. My recollections of these days at Ramah are pleasant ones.

Philippus Inglavina and Ludwig Alasua, two Eskimos, were engaged to hold themselves in readiness with their team of twelve dogs for a bright and early start for Hebron on the first clear morning. On the fourth morning after our arrival they announced that the weather was sufficiently clear for them to find their way over the hills. Mrs. Schmidt and Mrs. Filsehke filled an earthen jug with hot coffee and wrapped it, with some sandwiches, in a bearskin to keep from freezing for a few hours; sufficient wood to boil the kettle that night and the next morning was lashed with our baggage on the komatik; the Eskimos each received the daily ration of a plug of tobacco and a box of matches, which they demand when traveling, and then we said good-by and started. The komatik was loaded with Eskimos, and the rest of the native population trailed after us on foot. It is the custom on the coast for the people to accompany a komatik starting on a journey for some distance from the station.

The wind, which had died nearly out in the night, was rising again. It was directly in our teeth and shifting the loose snow unpleasantly. We had not gone far when one of the trailing Eskimos came running after us and shouting to our driver to stop. We halted, and when he overtook us he called the attention of Philippus to a high mountain known as Attanuek (the King), whose peak was nearly hidden by drifting snow. A consultation decided them that it would be dangerous to attempt the passes that day, and to our chagrin the Eskimos turned the dogs back to the station.

The next morning Attanuek's head was clear, the wind was light, the atmosphere bitter cold, and we were off in good season. We soon reached "Lamson's Hill," rising three thousand feet across our path, and shortly after daylight began the wearisome ascent, helping the dogs haul the komatik up steep places and wallowing through deep snow banks. Before noon one of our dogs gave out, and we had to cut him loose. An hour later we met George Ford on his way home to Nachvak from Davis Inlet, and some Eskimos with a team from the Hebron Mission, and from this latter team we borrowed a dog to take the place of the one that we had lost. Ford told us that his leader had gone mad that morning and he had been compelled to shoot it. He also in- formed me that wolves had followed him all the way from Okak to Hebron, mingling with his dogs at night, but at Hebron had left his trail.

At three o'clock we reached the summit of Lamson's Hill and

began the perilous descent, where only the most expert maneuvering on the part of the Eskimos saved our komatik from being smashed. In many places we had to let the sledge down over steep places, after first removing the dogs, and it was a good while after dark when we reached the bottom. Then, after working the komatik over a mile of rough boulders from which the wind had swept the snow, we at length came upon the sea ice of Saglak Bay, and at eight o'clock drew up at an igloosoak on an island several miles from the mainland.

This igloosoak was practically an underground dwelling, and the entrance was through a snow tunnel. From a single seal-gut window a dim light shone, but there was no other sign of human life. I groped my way into the tunnel, bent half double, stepping upon and stumbling over numerous dogs that blocked the way, and at the farther end bumped into a door. Upon pushing this open I found myself in a room perhaps twelve by fourteen feet in size. Three stone lamps shed a gloomy half-light over the place, and revealed a low bunk, covered with sealskins, extending along two sides of the room, upon which nine Eskimos--men, women and children--were lying. A half inch of soft slush covered the floor. The whole place was reeking in filth, infested with vermin, and the stench was sickening.

The people arose and welcomed us as Eskimos always do, most cordially. Our two drivers, who followed me with the wood we had brought, made a fire in a small sheet-iron tent stove kept in the shack by the missionaries for their use when traveling, and on it we placed our kettle full of ice for tea, and our sandwiches to thaw, for they were frozen as hard as bullets. One of the old women was half dead with consumption, and constantly spitting, and when we saw her turning our sandwiches on the stove our appetite appreciably diminished.

At Ramah I had purchased some dried caplin for dog food for the night. The caplin is a small fish, about the size of a smelt or a little larger, and is caught in the neighborhood of Hamilton Inlet and south. They are brought north by the missionaries to use for dog food when traveling in the winter, as they are more easily packed on the komatik than seal meat. The Eskimos are exceedingly fond of these dried fish, and they appealed to our men as too great a delicacy to waste upon the dogs. Therefore when feeding time came, seal blubber, of which there was an abundant supply in the igloo, fell to the lot of the animals, while our drivers and hosts appropriated the caplin to themselves. The bag of fish was placed in the center, with a dish of raw seal fat alongside, with the men, women and children surrounding it, and they were still banqueting upon the fish and fat when I, weary with traveling, fell asleep in my bag.

It was not yet dark the next evening when we came in sight of the Eskimo village at the Hebron mission, and the whole population of one hundred and eighty people and two hundred dogs, the former shouting, the latter howling, turned out to greet us. Several of the young men, fleeter of foot than the others, ran out on the ice, and when they had come near enough to see who we were, turned and ran back again ahead of our dogs, shouting "Kablunot! Kablunot!" (outlanders), and so, in the midst of pandemonium, we drew into the station, and received from the missionaries a most cordial welcome.

Here I was fortunate in securing for the next eighty miles of our journey an Eskimo with an exceptionally fine team of fourteen dogs. This new driver--Cornelius was his name--made my heart glad by consenting to travel without an attendant. I was pleased at this be- cause experience had taught me that each additional man meant just so much slower progress.

No time was lost at Hebron, for the weather was fine, and early morning found us on our way. At Napartok we reached the "first wood," and the sight of a grove of green spruce tops above the snow seemed almost like a glimpse of home.

It was dreary, tiresome work, this daily plodding southward over the endless snow, sometimes upon the wide ice field, sometimes crossing necks of land with tedious ascents and dangerous descents of hills, making no halt while daylight lasted, save to clear the dogs' entangled traces and snatch a piece of hard-tack for a cheerless luncheon.

Okak, two days' travel south of Hebron, with a population of three hundred and twenty-nine, is the largest Eskimo village in Labrador and an important station of the Moravian missionaries. Besides the chapel, living apartments and store of the mission a neat, well- organized little hospital has just been opened by them and placed in charge of Dr. S. Hutton, an English physician. Young, capable and with every prospect of success at home, he and his charming wife have resigned all to

185

come to the dreary Labrador and give their lives and efforts to the uplifting of this bit of benighted humanity.

We were entertained by the doctor and Mrs. Hutton and found them most delightful people. The only other member of the hospital corps was Miss S. Francis, a young woman who has prepared herself as a trained nurse to give her life to the service. I had an opportunity to visit with Dr. Hutton several of the Eskimo dwellings, and was struck by their cleanliness and the great advance toward civilization these people have made over their northern kinsmen. We had now reached a section where timber grows, and some of the houses were quite pretentious for the frontier--well furnished, of two or three rooms, and far superior to many of the homes of the outer coast breeds to the south. This, of course, is the visible result of the century of Moravian labors. Here I engaged, with the aid of the missionaries, Paulus Avalar and Boas Anton with twelve dogs to go with us to Nain, and after one day at Okak our march was resumed.

It is a hundred miles from Okak to Nain and on the way the Kiglapait Mountain must be crossed, as the Atlantic ice outside is liable to be shattered at any time should an easterly gale blow, and there is no possible retreat and no opportunity to escape should one be caught upon it at such a time, as perpendicular cliffs rise sheer from the sea ice here.

We had not reached the summit of the Kiglapait when night drove us into camp in a snow igloo. The Eskimos here are losing the art of snow-house building, and this one was very poorly constructed, and, with a temperature of thirty or forty degrees below zero, very cold and uncomfortable.

When we turned into our sleeping bags Paulus, who could talk a few words of English, remarked to me: "Clouds say big snow maybe. Here very bad. No dog feed. We go early," and pointing to my watch face indicated that we should start at midnight. At eleven o'clock I heard him and Boas get up and go out. Half an hour later they came back with a kettle of hot tea and we had breakfast. Then the two Eskimos, by candlelight read aloud in their language a form of worship and sang a hymn. All along the coast between Hebron and Makkovik I found morning and evening worship and grace before and after meals a regular institution with the Eskimos, whose religious training is carefully looked after by the Moravians.

By midnight our komatik was packed. "Ooisht! ooisht!" started the dogs forward as the first feathery flakes of the threatened storm fell lazily down. Not a breath of wind was stirring and no sound broke the ominous silence of the night save the crunch of our feet on the snow and the voice of the driver urging on the dogs.

Boas went ahead, leading the team on the trail. Presently he halted and shouted back that he could not make out the landmarks in the now thickening snow. Then we circled about until an old track was found and went on again. Time and again this maneuver was repeated. The snow now began to fall heavily and the wind rose.

No further sign of the track could be discovered and short halts were made while Paulus examined my compass to get his bearings.

Finally the summit of the Kiglapait was reached, and the descent was more rapid. At one place on a sharp down grade the dogs started on a run and we jumped upon the komatik to ride. Moving at a rapid pace the team, dimly visible ahead, suddenly disappeared. Paulus rolled off the komatik to avoid going over the ledge ahead, but the rest of us had no time to jump, and a moment later the bottom fell out of our track and we felt ourselves dropping through space. It was a fall of only fifteen feet, but in the night it seemed a hundred. Fortunately we landed on soft snow and no harm was done, but we had a good shaking up.

The storm grew in force with the coming of daylight. Forging on through the driving snow we reached the ocean ice early in the forenoon and at four o'clock in the afternoon the shelter of an Eskimo hut.

The storm was so severe the next morning our Eskimos said to venture out in it would probably mean to get lost, but before noon the wind so far abated that we started.

The snow fell thickly all day, the wind began to rise again, and a little after four o'clock the real force of the gale struck us in one continued, terrific sweep, and the snow blew so thick that we nearly smothered. The temperature was thirty degrees below zero. We could not see the length of the komatik. We did not dare let go of it, for had we separated ourselves a half dozen yards we should certainly have been lost.

Somehow the instincts of drivers and dogs, guided by the hand of a good Providence, led us to the mission house at Nain, which we reached at five o'clock and were overwhelmed by the kindness of the Moravians. This is the Moravian headquarters in Labrador, and the Bishop, Right Reverend A. Martin, with his aids, is in charge.

It was Saturday night when we reached Nain, and Sunday was spent here while we secured new drivers and dogs and waited for the storm to blow over.

Everyone was so cordial and hospitable that I almost regretted the necessity of leaving on Monday morning. The day was excessively cold and a head wind froze cheeks and noses and required an almost constant application of the hand to thaw them out and prevent them from freezing permanently. Easton even frosted his elbow through his heavy clothing of reindeer skin.

During the second day from Nain we met Missionary Christian Schmitt returning from a visit to the natives farther south, and on the ice had a half hour's chat.

That evening we reached Davis Inlet Post of the Hudson's Bay Company, and spent the night with Mr. Guy, the agent, and the following morning headed southward again, passed Cape Harrigan, and in another two days reached Hopedale Mission, where we arrived just ahead of one of the fierce storms* so frequent here at this season of the year, which held us prisoners from Thursday night until Monday morning. Two days later we pulled in at Makkovik, the last station of the Moravians on our southern trail.

* Since writing the above I have learned that a half-breed whom I met at Davis Inlet, his wife and a young native left that point for Hope- dale just after us, were overtaken by this storm, lost their way, and were probably overcome by the elements. Their dogs ate the bodies and a week later returned, well fed, to Davis Inlet. Dr. Grenfell found the bones in the spring.

Chapter 23: Back to Northwest River

We had now reached an English-speaking country; that is, a section where everyone talked understandable English, though at the same time nearly everyone was conversant with the Eskimo language.

All down the coast we had been fortunate in securing dogs and drivers with little trouble through the intervention of the missionaries; but at Makkovik dogs were scarce, and it seemed for a time as though we were stranded here, but finally, with missionary Townley's aid I engaged an old Eskimo named Martin Tuktusini to go with us to Rigolet. When I looked at Martin's dogs, however, I saw at once that they were not equal to the journey, unaided. Neither had I much faith in Martin, for he was an old man who had nearly reached the end of his usefulness.

A day was lost in vainly looking around for additional dogs, and then Mr. Townley generously loaned us his team and driver to help us on to Big Bight, fifteen miles away, where he thought we might get dogs to supplement Martin's.

At Big Bight we found a miserable hut, where the people were indescribably poor and dirty. A team was engaged after some delay to carry us to Tishialuk, thirty miles farther on our journey, which place we reached the following day at eleven o'clock.

There is a single hovel at Tishialuk, occupied by two brothers--John and Sam Cove--and their sister. Their only food was flour, and a limited quantity of that. Even tea and molasses, usually found amongst the "livyeres" (live-heres) of the coast, were lacking. Sam was only too glad of the opportunity to earn a few dollars, and was engaged with his team to join forces with Martin as far as Rigolet.

There are two routes from Tishialuk to Rigolet. One is the "Big Neck" route over the hills, and much shorter than the other, which is known as the outside route, though it also crosses a wide neck of land inside of Cape Harrison, ending at Pottle's Bay on Hamilton Inlet. It was my intention to take the Big Neck trail, but Martin strenuously opposed it on the ground that it passed over high hills, was much more difficult, and the probabilities of getting lost should a storm occur were much greater by that route than by the other. His objections prevailed, and upon the afternoon of the day after our arrival Sam was ready, and in a gale of wind we ran down on the ice to Tom Bromfield's cabin at Tilt Cove, that we might be ready to make an early start for Pottle's Bay the following morning, as the whole day would be needed to cross the neck of land to Pottle's Bay and the neatest shelter beyond.

Tom is a prosperous and ambitious hunter, and is fairly well-to-do as it goes on the Labrador. His one-room cabin was very comfortable, and he treated us to unwonted luxuries, such as butter, marmalade, and sugar for our tea.

During the evening he displayed to me the skin of a large wolf which he had killed a few days before, and told us the story of the killing.

"I were away, sir," related he, "wi' the dogs, savin' one which I leaves to home, 'tendin' my fox traps. The woman (meaning his wife) were alone wi' the young ones. In the evenin' (afternoon) her hears a fightin' of dogs outside, an' thinkin' one of the team was broke loose an' run home, she starts to go out to beat the beasts an' put a stop to the fightin'. But lookin' out first before she goes, what does she see but the wolf that owned that skin, and right handy to the door he were, too. He were a big divil, as you sees, sir. She were scared. Her tries to take down the rifle-- the one as is there on the pegs, sir. The wolf and the dog be now fightin' agin' the door, and she thinks they's handy to breakin' in, and it makes her a bit shaky in the hands, and she makes a slip and the rifle he goes off bang! makin' that hole there marrin' the timber above the windy. Then the wolf he goes off too; he be scared at the shootin'. When I comes home she tells me, and I lays fur the beast. 'Twere the next day and I were in the house when I hears the dogs fightin' and I peers out the windy, and there I sees the wolf fightin' wi' the dogs, quite handy by the house. Well, sir, I just gits the rifle down and goes out, and when the dogs sees me they runs and leaves the wolf, and I up and knocks he over wi' a bullet, and there's his skin, worth a good four dollars, for he be an extra fine one, sir."

We sat up late that night listening to Tom's stories.

The next morning was leaden gray, and promised snow. With the hope of reaching Pottle's Bay before dark we started forward early, and at one o'clock in the afternoon were in the soft snow of the spruce-covered neck. Traveling was very bad and progress so slow that darkness found us still amongst the scrubby firs. Martin and I walked ahead of the dogs, making a path and cutting away the growth where it was too thick to permit the passage of the teams.

Martin was guiding us by so circuitous a path that finally I began to suspect he had lost his way, and, calling a halt, suggested that we had better make a shelter and stop until daylight, particularly as the snow was now falling. When you are lost in the bush it is a good rule to stop where you are until you make certain of your course. Martin in this instance, however, seemed very positive that we were going in the right direction, though off the usual trail, and he said that in another hour or so we would certainly come out and find the salt-water ice of Hamilton Inlet. So after an argument I agreed to proceed and trust in his assurances.

Easton, who was driving the rear team, was completely tired out with the exertion of steering the komatik through the brush and untangling the dogs, which seemed to take a delight in spreading out and getting their traces fast around the numerous small trees, and I went to the rear to relieve him for a time from the exhausting work.

It was nearly two o'clock in the morning when we at length came upon the ice of a brook which Martin admitted he had never seen before and confessed that he was completely lost. I ordered a halt at once until daylight. We drank some cold water, ate some hard-tack and then stretched our sleeping bags upon the snow and, all of us weary, lay down to let the drift cover us while we slept.

At dawn we were up, and with a bit of jerked venison in my

hand to serve for breakfast, I left the others to lash the load on the komatiks and follow me and started on ahead. I had walked but half a mile when I came upon the rough hummocks of the Inlet ice. Before noon we found shelter from the now heavily driving snowstorm in a livyere's hut and here remained until the following morning.

Just beyond this point, in crossing a neck of land, we came upon a small hut and, as is usual on the Labrador, stopped for a moment. The people of the coast always expect travelers to stop and have a cup of tea with them, and feel that they have been slighted if this is not done. Here I found a widow named Newell, whom I knew, and her two or three small children. It was a miserable hut, without even the ordinary comforts of the poorer coast cabins, only one side of the earthen floor partially covered with rough boards, and the people destitute of food. Mrs. Newell told me that the other livyeres were giving her what little they had to eat, and had saved them during the winter from actual starvation. I had some hardtack and tea in my "grub bag," and these I left with her.

Two days later we pulled in at Rigolet and were greeted by my friend Fraser. It was almost like getting home again, for now I was on old, familiar ground. A good budget of letters that had come during the previous summer awaited us and how eagerly we read them! This was the first communication we had received from our home folks since the previous June and it was now February twenty-first.

We rested with Fraser until the twenty-third, and then with Mark Pallesser, a Groswater Bay Eskimo, turned in to Northwest River where Stanton, upon coming from the interior, had remained to wait for our return that he might join us for the balance of the journey out. The going was fearful and snowshoeing in the heavy snow tiresome. It required two days to reach Mulligan, where we spent the night with skipper Tom Blake, one of my good old friends, and at Tom's we feasted on the first fresh venison we had had since leaving the Ungava district. In the whole distance from Whale River not a caribou had been killed during the winter by any one, while in the previous winter a single hunter at Davis Inlet shot in one day a hundred and fifty, and only ceased then because he had no more ammunition. Tom had killed three or four, and south of

192

this point I learned of a hunter now and then getting one.

Northwest River was reached on Monday, February twenty-sixth, and we took Cotter by complete surprise, for he had not expected us for another month.

The day after our arrival Stanton came to the Post from a cabin three miles above, where he had been living alone, and he was delighted to see us.

The lumbermen at Muddy Lake, twenty miles away, heard of our arrival and sent down a special messenger with a large addition to the mail which I was carrying out and which had been growing steadily in bulk with its accumulations at every station.

This is the stormiest season of the year in Labrador, and weather conditions were such that it was not until March sixth that we were permitted to resume our journey homeward.

Chapter 24: The End of the Long Trail

The storm left the ice covered with a depth of soft snow into which the dogs sank deep and hauled the komatik with difficulty. Snowshoeing, too, was unusually hard. The day we left Northwest River (Tuesday, March sixth) the temperature rose above the freezing point, and when it froze that night a thin crust formed, through which our snowshoes broke, adding very materially to the labor of walking--and of course it was all walking.

As the days lengthened and the sun asserting his power, pushed higher and higher above the horizon, the glare upon the white expanse of snow dazzled our eyes, and we had to put on smoked glasses to protect ourselves from snow-blindness. Even with the glasses our driver, Mark, became partially snow-blind, and when, on the evening of the third day after leaving Northwest River, we reached his home at Karwalla, an Eskimo settlement a few miles west of Rigolet, it became necessary for us to halt until he was sufficiently recovered to enable him to travel again.

Here we met some of the Eskimos that had been connected with the Eskimo village at the World's Fair at Chicago, in 1893. Mary, Mark's wife, was one of the number. She told me of having been exhibited as far west as Portland, Oregon, and I asked:

"Mary, aren't you discontented here, after seeing so much of the world? Wouldn't you like to go back?"

"No, sir," she answered. "'Tis fine here, where I has plenty of company. 'Tis too lonesome in the States, sir."

"But you can't get the good things to eat here--the fruits and other things," I insisted.

"I likes the oranges and apples fine, sir--but they has no seal meat or deer's meat in the States."

It was not until Tuesday, March thirteenth, three days after our arrival at Karwalla, that Mark thought himself quite able to proceed. The brief "mild" gave place to intense cold and blustery, snowy weather. We pushed on toward West Bay, on the outer coast again, by the "Backway," an arm of Hamilton Inlet that extends almost due east from Karwalla.

At West Bay I secured fresh dogs to carry us on to Cartwright, which I hoped to reach in one day more. But the going was fearfully poor, soft snow was drifted deep in the trail over Cape Porcupine, the ice in Traymore was broken up by the gales, and this necessitated a long detour, so it was nearly dark and snowing hard when we at last reached the house of James Williams, at North River, just across Sandwich Bay from Cartwright Post. The greeting I received was so kindly that I was not altogether disappointed at having to spend the night here.

"We've been expectin' you all winter, sir," said Mrs. Williams. "When you stopped two years ago you said you'd come some other time, and we knew you would. 'Tis fine to see you again, sir."

On the afternoon of March seventeenth we reached Cartwright Post of the Hudson's Bay Company, and my friend Mr. Ernest Swaffield, the agent, and Mrs. Swaffield, who had been so kind to me on my former trip, gave us a cordial welcome. Here also I met Dr. Mumford, the resident physician at Dr. Grenfell's mission hospital at Battle Harbor, who was on a trip along the coast visiting the sick.

Another four days' delay was necessary at Cartwright before dogs could be found to carry us on, but with Swaffield's aid I finally secured teams and we resumed our journey, stopping at night at the native cabins along the route. Much bad weather was encountered to retard us and I had difficulty now and again in securing dogs and drivers. Many of the men that I had on my previous trip, when I brought Hubbard's body out to Battle Harbor, were absent hunting, but whenever I could find them they invariably engaged with me again to help me a stage upon the journey.

From Long Pond, near Seal Islands, neither I nor the men I

195

had knew the way (when I traveled down the coast on the former occasion my drivers took a route outside of Long Pond), and that afternoon we went astray, and with no one to set us right wandered about upon the ice until long after dark, looking for a hut at Whale Bight, which was finally located by the dogs smelling smoke and going to it.

A little beyond Whale Bight we came upon a bay that I recognized, and from that point I knew the trail and headed directly to Williams' Harbor, where I found John and James Russell, two of my old drivers, ready to take us on to Battle Harbor.

At last, on the afternoon of March twenty-sixth we reached the hospital, and how good it seemed to be back almost within touch of civilization. It was here that I ended that long and dreary sledge journey with the last remains of dear old Hubbard, in the spring of 1904, and what a flood of recollections came to me as I stood in front of the hospital and looked again across the ice of St. Lewis Inlet! How well I remembered those weary days over there at Fox Harbor, watching the broken, heaving ice that separated me from Battle Island; the little boat that one day came into the ice and worked its way slowly through it until it reached us and took us to the hospital and the ship; and how thankful I felt that I had reached here with my precious burden safe.

Mrs. Mumford made us most welcome, and entertained me in the doctor's house, and was as good and kind as she could be.

I must again express my appreciation of the truly wonderful work that Dr. Grenfell and his brave associates are carrying on amongst the people of this dreary coast. Year after year, they brave the hardships and dangers of sea and fog and winter storms that they may minister to the lowly and needy in the Master's name. It is a saying on the coast that "even the dogs know Dr. Grenfell," and it is literally true, for his activities carry him everywhere and God knows what would become of some of the people if he were not there to look after them. His practice extends over a larger territory than that of any other physician in the world, but the only fee he ever collects is the pleasure that comes with the knowledge of work well done.

At Battle Harbor I was told by a trader that it would be difficult, if not impossible, to procure dogs to carry us up the Straits toward Quebec, and I was strongly advised to end my snowshoe and dog journey here and wait for a steamer that was expected to come in April to the whaling station at Cape Charles, twelve miles away. This seemed good advice, for if we could get a steamer here within three weeks or so that would take us to St. Johns we should reach home probably earlier than we possibly could by going to Quebec.

There is a government coast telegraph line that follows the north shore of the St. Lawrence from Quebec to Chateau Bay, but the nearest office open at this time was at Red Bay, sixty-five miles from Battle Harbor, and I determined to go there and get into communication with home and at the same time telegraph to Bowring Brothers in St. Johns and ascertain from them exactly when I might expect the whaling steamer.

William Murphy offered to carry me over with his team, and, leaving Stanton and Easton comfortably housed at Battle Harbor and both of them quite content to end their dog traveling here, on the morning after my arrival Murphy and I made an early start for Red Bay.

Except in the more sheltered places the bay ice had broken away along the Straits and we had to follow the rough ice barricades, sometimes working inland up and down the rocky hills and steep grades. Before noon we passed Henley Harbor and the Devil's Dining Table--a basaltic rock formation--and a little later reached Chateau Bay and had dinner in a native house. Beyond this point there are cabins built at intervals of a few miles as shelter for the linemen when making repairs to the wire. We passed one of these at Wreck Cove toward evening, but as a storm was threatening, pushed on to the next one at Green Bay, fifty-five miles from Battle Harbor. It was dark before we got there, and to reach the Bay we had to descend a steep hill. I shall never forget the ride down that hill. It is very well to go over places like that when you know the way and what you are likely to bring up against, but I did not know the way and had to pin my faith blindly on Murphy, who had taken me over rotten ice during the day--- ice that waved up and down with our weight and sometimes broke behind us. My opinion of him was that he was a reckless devil, and when we began to descend that hill, five hundred feet to the bay ice, this opinion was strengthened. I would have said uncomplimentary things to him had time permitted. I expected anything to happen. It looked in the night as though a sheer precipice with a bottomless pit below was in front of us. Two drags were thrown over the komatik runners to hold us back, but in spite of them we went like a shot out of a gun, he on one side, I on the other, sticking our heels into the hard snow as we extended our legs ahead, trying our best to hold back and stop our wild progress. But, much to my surprise, when we got there, and I verily believe to Murphy's surprise also, we landed right side up at the bottom, with no bones broken. There were three men camped in the shack here, and we spent the night with them.

Early the next day we reached Red Bay and the telegraph office. There are no words in the English language adequate to express my feelings of gratification when I heard the instruments clicking off the messages. It had been seventeen years since I had handled a telegraph key--when I was a railroad telegrapher down in New England--and how I fondled that key, and what music the click of the sounder was to my ears!

My messages were soon sent, and then I sat down to wait for the replies.

The office was in the house of Thomas Moors, and he was good enough to invite me to stop with him while in Red Bay. His daughter was the telegraph operator.

The next day the answers to my telegrams came, and many messages from friends, and one from Bowring & Company stating that no steamer would be sent to Cape Charles. I had been making inquiries here, however, in the meantime, and learned that it was quite possible to secure dogs and continue the journey up the north shore, so I was not greatly disappointed. I dispatched Murphy at once to Battle Harbor to bring on the other men, waiting myself at Red Bay for their coming, and holding teams in readiness for an immediate departure when they should arrive.

They drove in at two o'clock on April fourth, and we left at once. On the morning of the sixth we passed through Blanc Sablon, the boundary line between Newfoundland and Canadian territory, and here I left the Newfoundland letters from my mail bag. From this point the majority of the natives are Acadians, and speak only French.

At Brador Bay I stopped to telegraph. No operator was there, so I sent the message myself, left the money on the desk and proceeded.

Three days more took us to St. Augustine Post of the Hudson's Bay Company, where we arrived in the morning and accepted the hospitality of Burgess, the Agent.

Our old friends the Indians whom we met on our inland trip at Northwest River were here, and John, who had eaten supper with us at our camp on the hill on the first portage, expressed great pleasure at meeting us, and had many questions to ask about the country. They had failed in their deer hunt, and had come out half-starved a week or so before, from the interior.

We did fifty miles on the eleventh, changing dogs at Harrington at noon and running on to Sealnet Cove that night. Here we found more Indians who had just emerged from the interior, driven to the coast for food like those at St. Augustine as the result of their failure to find caribou.

Two days later we reached the Post at Romain, and on the afternoon of April seventeenth reached Natashquan and open water. Here I engaged passage on a small schooner--the first afloat in the St. Lawrence--to take us on to Eskimo Point, seventy miles farther, where the Quebec steamer, King Edward, was expected to arrive in a week or so. That night we boarded the schooner and sailed at once. Into the sea I threw the clothes I had been wearing, and donned fresh ones. What a relief it was to be clear of the innumerable horde "o' wee sma' beasties" that had been my close companions all the way down from the Eskimo igloos in the North. I have wondered many times since whether those clothes swam ashore, and if they did what happened to them.

It was a great pleasure to be upon the water again, and see the shore slip past, and feel that no more snowstorms, no more bitter northern blasts, no more hungry days and nights were to be faced.

Since June twenty-fifth, the day we dipped our paddles into the water of Northwest River and turned northward into the wastes of the great unknown wilderness, eight hundred miles had been traversed in reaching Fort Chimo, and on our return journey with dogs and komatik and snowshoes, two thousand more.

We reached Eskimo Point on April twentieth, and that very day a rain began that turned the world into a sea of slush. I was glad indeed that our komatik work was finished, for it would now have been very difficult, if not impossible, to travel farther with dogs.

I at once deposited in the post office the bag of letters that I had carried all the way from far-off Ungava. This was the first mail that any single messenger had ever carried by dog train from that distant point, and I felt quite puffed up with the honor of it.

The week that we waited here for the King Edward was a dismal one, and when the ship finally arrived we lost no time in getting ourselves and our belongings aboard. It was a mighty satisfaction to feel the pulse of the engines that with every revolution took us nearer home, and when at last we tied up at the steamer's wharf in Quebec, I heaved a sigh of relief.

On April thirtieth, after an absence of just eleven months, we found ourselves again in the whirl and racket of New York. The portages and rapids and camp fires, the Indian wigwams and Eskimo igloos and the great, silent white world of the North that we had so recently left were now only memories. We had reached the end of The Long Trail. The work of exploration begun by Hubbard was finished.

Appendix

Labrador Plants

Specimens collected along the route of the expedition between Northwest River and Lake Michikamau. Determined at the New York Botanical Gardens:

Ledum groonlandicum, Oeder. Comarum palustre L. Rubus arcticus L. Solidago multiradiata. Ait. Sanguisorba Canadensis L. Linnaea Americana, Forbes. Dasiphora fruticosa (L), Rydb. Chamnaerion latifolium (L), Sweet. Viburnum pancifloram, Pylaim. Viscaxia alpina (L), Roehl. Menyanthes trifoliata L. Vaznera trifolia (L), Morong. Ledum prostratum, Rotlb. Betula glandulosa, Michx. Kalmia angustifolia. Aronia nigra (Willd), Britt. Comus Canadensis L. Arenaria groenlandica (Retz), Spreng. Barbarea stricta, Audry. Eriophorum russeolum, Fries. Eriophorum polystachyon L. Phegopteris Phegopt@ (L), Fee.

Lichens

Cladonia deformis (L), Hoffen. Alectoria dehrolenea (Ehrh.), Nyl. Umbilicaria Neuhlenbergii (Ac L.), Tuck.

Geological Notes

By G. M. Richards All bearings given, refer to the true meridian.
My sincere thanks are due Prof. J.F. Kemp and Dr. C.P.

Berkey, whose generous assistance has made this work possible.

Route Followed

The route was by steamer to the head of Hamilton Inlet, Labrador-- thence by canoes up Grand Lake and the Nascaupee River. Fifteen miles above Grand Lake, a portage route was followed which makes a long detour through a series of lakes to avoid rapids in the river. This trail again returns to the Nascaupee River at Seal Lake and for some fifty miles above Seal Lake, follows the river. It then leaves the Nascaupee, making a second long detour through lakes to the north. On one of these lakes (Bibiquasin Lake) the trail was lost, and thereafter we traveled in a westerly direction until reaching Lake Michikamau.

Our food supply was then in so depleted a condition the party was obliged to separate, three of us returning to Northwest River.

It will be understood that the circumstances would allow of but a very limited examination of the geological features of the country. Only typical rock specimens, or those whose character was at all doubtful were brought back.

Previous Exploration

Mr. A.P. Low penetrated to Lake Michikamau, by way of the Grand River. He has thoroughly described the lake in his report to the Canadian Geological Survey, 1895, and it is not touched upon in the following paper. In the summer of 1903, an expedition led by Leonidas Hubbard, Jr., attempted to reach Lake Michikamau by ascending the Nascaupee River; they, however, missed the mouth of that stream on Grand Lake and followed the Susan River instead, pursuing a northwesterly course for two months without reaching the lake. On the return journey, Mr. Hubbard died of starvation, his two companions, Mr. Wallace and a half-breed Indian, barely escaping a similar fate.

Geographical Results of the Expedition

The Northwest River represented on the map of the Canadian Geological Survey (made from information obtained from the Indians) as draining Lake Michikamau, is but three and one-half miles long, and connects Grand Lake with Hamilton Inlet. There are six streams flowing into Grand Lake, instead of only one. It is the Nascaupee River that flows from Lake Michikamau to Grand Lake; and Seal Lake instead of being the source of the Nascaupee River is merely an expansion of it.

The source of the Crooked River was also discovered and mapped, as well as a great number of smaller lakes.

On the Northern Slope the George and Koroksoak Rivers and several lakes were mapped, and some smaller rivers located.

Detailed Description of Route Explored

Northwest River which flows into a small sandy bay at the head of Hamilton Inlet is only three and one-half miles long and drains Grand Lake.

For one-quarter of a mile above its mouth the river maintains an average width of one hundred and fifty yards, and a depth of two and one-half fathoms. It then expands into a shallow sheet of water two miles wide and three miles long, known locally as "The Little Lake." At the head of this small expansion the river again contracts where it flows out of Grand Lake. This point is known as "The Rapids," and although there is a strong current, the stream may be ascended in canoes without tracking.

At the foot of "The Rapids" the effect of the spring tides is barely perceptible. Between Grand Lake and the head of Hamilton Inlet, Northwest River flows through a deposit of sand marked by several distinct marine terraces.

Grand Lake is a body of fresh water forty miles long and from two to six miles in width, having a direction N. 75 degrees W. It lies in a deep valley between rocky hills that rise to a height of about four hundred feet above the lake, and was doubtless at one time an extension of Hamilton Inlet. At Cape Corbeau and Berry Head the rocks rise almost perpendicularly from the water; at the former place, to a height of three hundred feet.

203

Except in a few places the hills are covered to their summits by a thick growth of small spruce and fir.

At the head of the lake there are two bays, one extending slightly to the southwest, the other nearly due north. Into the former flow the Susan and Beaver Rivers, while into the latter empties the water of the Nascaupee and Crooked Rivers. Besides these there are two small streams, the Cape Corbeau River on the south, and Watty's Brook on the north shore.

At the point where the Nascaupee and Crooked Rivers enter the lake there are two low islands of sand, and a great deal of sand is being carried down by the two streams and deposited in the lake, which is very shallow for some distance from the shore.

Three miles above the mouth of the Nascaupee River it is separated from the Crooked River by a plain of stratified sand and gravel, three-quarters of a mile wide, with two well-defined terraces. The first is twenty feet above the river and extends back some three hundred yards to a second terrace, rising seventy-five feet above the first.

Half way between this terrace and the Crooked River is, the old bed of the Nascaupee River, nearly parallel to its present course. A similar abandoned channel curve was found, making a small arc to the south of the Crooked River.

Above Grand Lake the Nascaupee River flows through an ancient valley, which is from a few hundred yards to a mile wide and cut deep into the old Archaean rocks, affording an excellent example of river erosion. The banks are of sand, and in some places clay, extending back to the foot of the precipitous hills. Apparently the ancient river valley has been partly filled with drift, down through which the river has cut its way; the present bed of the stream being of post glacial formation. The general direction of the river is N. 83 degrees W.

Fifteen miles above Grand Lake, the Red River joins the main stream, coming from N. 87 degrees W. Below its junction with the latter stream, the Nascaupee River has a width varying between two and three hundred yards, and an average depth of about ten feet.

The Red River is two hundred feet wide, and its water, unlike that of the main stream, has a red brown color, like that of many of the streams of Ontario which have their source in swamp or Muskeg lands.

The first rapids in the Red River are said to be eight miles above its mouth. Directly opposite the junction of the two streams the portage leaves the Nascaupee River. The direction is N. 24 degrees E. and the distance five and one-half miles, with an elevation of 1050 feet above the river at the end of the second mile.

The last three and one-half miles lead across a level tableland, to a small lake, from which the trail descends through two lakes into a shallow valley.

The entire country from the head of Grand Lake to this point has been devastated by fire, only a few trees near the water having escaped destruction, and the ground, except in a few places, is destitute even of its usual covering of reindeer moss.

The underlying rock is gneiss, and the country from the Nascaupee River is thickly strewn with huge glacial boulders.

The majority of these boulders have been derived from the immediate vicinity, but many consisting of a coarse pegmatite carrying considerable quantities of ilmenite were observed. None of this rock was seen in place.

The valley last mentioned is separated from the Crooked River by Caribou Ridge, a broad, flat-topped elevation, three hundred and fifty feet high, dotted by small lakes, which fill almost every appreciable depression in the rock.

The general course to the Crooked River is northeast; at the point where the portage reaches it the stream is fifty yards wide and very shallow; flowing over a bed of coarse drift, which obstructs the river, forming a series of small lake expansions with rapids at the outlet of each. Between Grand Lake and the point where we reached the river, the Indians say it is not navigable in canoes, owing to rapids.

The Crooked River has its source in Lake Nipishish, which is about twenty-two miles long, with an average width of three miles, and a course due north. Six miles above the outlet of the lake is a bay, five miles long, extending N. 80 degrees W.

Along the north shore of the lake and in the bay are several small islands of drift, and many huge angular boulders projecting above the water. The country in the vicinity of the lake and in the valley of the Crooked River is covered with mounds and ridges of drift and many small moraines.

These moraines consisting of boulders for the most part from the immediate vicinity, seemed to have no given direction, but were usually found at the ends of, and in a transverse direction to the ridges.

The trail leaves Lake Nipishish near the head of the large bay, continuing in a direction between north and northwest, through several insignificant lakes, all drained indirectly by the Crooked River, until it reached Otter Lake, which is eight miles long, running nearly north and south, and is five hundred and fifty feet below the summits of the surrounding hills.

From Otter Lake, the course is west through five diminutive lakes, and across a series of sandy ridges to a small shallow lake, which is the source of Babewendigash River. Between this lake and Seal Lake intervene a high range of mountains--the highest seen on the journey to Lake Michikamau--rising fully one thousand feet above the level of Seal Lake. They are visible for miles in any direction, and were seen from Caribou Ridge nearly a month before we reached them.

They are glaciated to their summits, which are entirely destitute of vegetation and in August were still, in places, covered with snow. Babewendigash River winds to and fro between the mountains, its course being determined to a great extent by esker ridges that follow it on either side and which are often more than one hundred feet high. Throughout its length of twenty-five miles there are five rapids and three small lake expansions.

Seal Lake, into which the river flows, is in part an expansion of the Nascaupee River and fills a basin surrounded on every side by mountains, rising several hundred feet above the water. The lake is comparatively shallow, and has a perceptible current. There are several small islands of drift, covered by a scanty growth of spruce and willow. The main lake has direction N. 45 degrees W., and is ten miles long and two and one-half miles wide. The northwestern arm is fifteen miles long, with the same width, and a course N. 80 degrees W.

The steep rocky shores have precluded the formation of terraces. Above Seal Lake the course of the Nascaupee River varies between N. 40 degrees W. and N. 80 degrees W.

Five miles above the lake there is an expansion of the river, called Wuchusk Nipi, or Muskrat Lake, which is eight miles long and a mile and a half wide, with a course N. 40 degrees W. Except for a channel along the western shore, the lake is very shallow, being nearly filled with sand carried down by the river. There is a small stream flowing into this lake expansion near its head, called Wuchusk Nipishish.

For fifty miles above Muskrat Lake, the river flows between sandy banks, marked on either side by two well-defined terraces. The river valley gradually becomes more narrow and the current stronger and with the exception of a few small expansions, progress is only possible by means of tracking. There are, however, in this distance but two rapids necessitating portages.

Opposite the point where the portage leaves the Nascaupee to make a second long detour around rapids, a small river flows in from the southwest, having a sheer fall of almost fifty feet, just above its junction with the main stream.

The trail, after leaving the river, has a course N. 35 degrees W. for two miles; it then turns N. 85 degrees W. six miles, and again N. 55 degrees W. four miles.

In its course are four small lakes, but there is an unbroken portage of eight miles between the last two. Nearly the whole country has been denuded by fire, and the prospect is desolate in the extreme. The end of the portage is on the high rolling plateau of the interior, timbered by a sparse and stunted second growth of spruce, covered everywhere with white reindeer moss, and strewn with lakes innumerable.

The trail which runs N. 50 degrees W. and has not been used for eight years, gradually became more and more indistinct, until on Bibiquasin Lake it disappeared entirely. Thereafter the course was N. 70 degrees W., and finally due west, through a series of lakes which at last brought us to Lake Michikamau. The largest of this series is Kasheshebogamog Lake, a sheet of water twenty-three miles long, but broken by numerous bays and countless islands of drift, with a direction S. 75 degrees W. The lake is confined between long boulder-covered ridges, and is fed at its western end by a small stream.

Although its outlet was not discovered, it doubtless drains into the Nascaupee River.

On the return journey an attempt was made to descend the Nascaupee River below Seal Lake.

The river leaves the lake at its southeastern extremity, flowing between hills that rise almost straight from the waters edge, and is one long continuation of heavy rapids. After following the stream for two days we were obliged to retrace our steps to Seal Lake, thereafter keeping to the course pursued on the inland journey.

Details of Rock Exposure

The numbers following the names of rocks refer to corresponding numbers in appendix.

Of the rocks observed, by far the greater number are foliated basic eruptives,--schists and gneisses. There are, however, some that are of undoubted sedimentary origin, but highly metamorphosed.

The general direction of foliation is a few degrees south of east, subject, of course, to many local changes.

Along Grand Lake the rock is a compact amphibolite [3] with a strike S. 78 degrees E. cut by numerous pegmatite dikes, having a strike N. 30 degrees W. and a dip 79 degrees W.. These dikes vary in width from three to twenty feet. Half way to the head of the lake is a dike [1] having a total width of eight feet, consisting of a central band of segregated quartz, six feet wide, cut by numerous thin sheets of biotite, which probably mark the planes of shearing. The quartz is bordered on either side by a band of orthoclase,' one foot in width. Between these bands of orthoclase and the neighboring amphibolite are narrow bands of schist [2]

One hundred feet south of the above point is a second dike having a similar strike and dip and a width of eighteen feet. A third narrow dike, containing small pockets of magnetite, is twenty-five feet south of the second. Only the first is distinguished by the segregation of the quartz.

The next outcrop observed was on the portage from the Nascaupee River. The rock, a biotite granite gneiss [4] having a strike N. 82 degrees E. is much weathered and split by the action of the frost, and marked by pockets of quartz, usually four or five inches in width.

Between this point and Lake Nipishish the underlying rock

differs only in being more extremely crushed and foliated. The one exception is on Caribou Ridge, which is capped by a much altered gabbro. [6]

The first noticeable change in the character of the country rock is a Washkagama Lake, where a fine grained epidotic schist [7] was observed, having a dip 82 degrees W. and a strike S. 78 degrees E.

At Otter Lake a much foliated and weathered phyllite [8] was found. Strike N. 73 degrees E. and a dip of 16 degrees.

On the Babewendigash River seven miles east of Seal Lake is an exposure of highly metamorphosed ancient sedimentary rocks. The outcrop occurs at a height of four hundred feet above the river; and there is a well-marked stratification.

The lowest bed of a calcarous sericitic schist [9] is four feet thick and underlies a bed of schistose lime stone [10] six feet in thickness, which is in turn covered by a finely laminated phyllite, [11] ten feet thick. The whole is capped by thirty feet of quartzite, [12] which forms the top of a long ridge.

Owing to the strong weathering action this thickness of quartzite is doubtless much less than it was originally.

Forty-six miles above Seal Lake an exposure of phyllite was seen, the same in every respect as the one east of Seal Lake, just mentioned.

The general direction of foliation is S. 70 degrees E. and the dip 70 degrees. The higher hills west of Seal Lake are capped by a much altered gabbro [13] that has undergone considerable weathering.

Between the Nascaupee River and a few miles beyond Bibiquasin Lake the rock is quartzite, [14] considerably weathered and covered by drift. Bowlders of this quartzite were seen along the Nascaupee River long before the first outcrop was reached, showing the general direction of the glacial movement to have been to the southeast. From Bibiquasin Lake to Lake Kasheshebogamog the country is covered with much drift; the only exposures are on the steep hillsides. The rock being a coarse hornblende granite.

The western end of Kasheshebogamog Lake lies within the limit of the anorthosite [15] area, which extends from that point to Lake Michikamau, a direct distance of twenty miles and was the only anorthosite observed on the journey.

Glacial Striae

First portage opposite Red River	S. 45 degrees E.
On Caribou Ridge	E.
At Washkagama Lake	S. 70 degrees E.
Near Seal Lake	N. 85 degrees E.
At Wuchusk Nipi	S. 75 degrees E.
Thirty-two miles above Wuchusk Nipi	S. 70 degrees E.

Microscopical Features of the Rock Specimens

By G. M. Richards, Columbia University 1--Pegmatite-Grand Lake. The specimen was taken from a pegmatite dike at its contact with an amphibolite. In the hand specimen it is an apparently pure orthoclase but in the thin section small scattered quartz grains are observed; as well as the alteration products, Kaolin and sericite.

The minerals at contact are quartz, biotite, magnetite and hornblende.

Both the quartz and orthoclase contain dust inclusions and crystallites, while the evidences of shearing and crushing are abundant.

2-Quartz Biotite Schist.

Contact between above dike and amphibolite. A coarse black rock carrying magnetite and pyrites in considerable quantities.

Under the microscope some of the biotite has a green coloration from decomposition and is surrounded by strong pleochroic halos.

Small grains of secondary pyroxene are numerous.

Amphibolite

3-Grand Lake.

A dark, compact rock, having a mottled appearance due to grains of plagioclase, and a green color in section.

Minerals present are hornblende, biotite, plagioclase, pyroxene, quartz and the alteration products from the feldspar.

The rock has been subjected to a strong crushing action, which has been resisted by only small portions of it. The spaces between the grains, which are intact, are filled with a confused mass of peripherally granulated minerals, in which strain shadows are very prominent.

The rock has been derived by dynamic metamorphism from a basic igneous rock.

4-Biotite Granite Gneiss.

Eighteen miles above mouth of Nascaupee River. A fine-grained rock of gneissic structure having a faint pink color.

Plagioclase, microcline and quartz are the predominating minerals, while biotite, titanite, epidote, apatite, zircon and garnet are present in smaller quantities.

There is also a small amount of hematite, pyroxene and sericite.

The rock, which is of a granitic composition, contains numerous crystallites and has been subjected to considerable strain and crushing, which has resulted in foliation.

5-Mica Granite Gneiss--Country Rock--near Caribou Ridge.

In the hand specimen the rock has the same appearance as No. 4, if anything, it is somewhat more compact.

The principal minerals are, plagioclase, biotite and microcline, with smaller quantities of quartz, iron oxide, pyroxene and garnet.

The feldspar is decomposed with the resulting formation of epidote, which is quite prominent. There are also numerous included crystals.

The rock has been greatly crushed and sheared, and is much finer than No. 4.

6--Cap of Caribou Ridge.

A hard compact rock of dark green color, having a mottled appearance, due to the presence of a white mineral.

Pyroxene, quartz and augite form the groundmass, as seen in section. There are a few small grains of magnetite,

The severe crushing to which the rock has been subjected has resulted in the conversion of the plagioclase into scapolite and also in the formation of zoisite by the characteristic alteration of the lime bearing silicate of the feldspar in conjunction with other constituents of the rock.

The light mineral is finely granulated and the whole is marked by uneven extinction.

The rock has probably been derived by dynamic metamorphism, from a coarse igneous rock like a gabbro.

7--Epidotic Sericitic Schist. Washkagama Lake.

A fine grained compact gray rock, of aggregate structure, consisting chiefly of quartz, plagioclase and biotite, and the alteration products epidote and sericite.

Under the microscope it is a confused mass of finely granulated minerals, with numerous included crystals.

The rock has undergone complete metamorphism and its origin is unknown.

8--Phyllite-Near Otter Lake.

A soft extremely fine grained gray rock, with a well developed schistose structure, carrying much magnetite, plagioclase, orthoclase and their alteration products.

The strain to which the rock has been subjected has resulted in a very fine lamination, and it is considerably weathered.

9--Calcarous Sericite Schist.--Seven Miles East of Seal Lake.

A dark compact rock, in which calcite and sericite predominate. Quartz is less plentiful. The results of shearing and pressure are very prominent and bring out the foliation, even in the calcite.

10--Schistose Limestone--Same location as No. 9.

A white rock having a peculiar mottled appearance due to the inclusions of decomposing biotite which project from the surrounding mass of calcite. There is some sericite present, also magnetite, resulting from the decomposition of the biotite.

The bent and metamorphosed condition of the calcite shows the shearing and crushing which the rock has undergone.

11--Phyllite--same location as No. 9.

A dark red, finely laminated rock consisting chiefly of decomposed biotite and feldspar, occasional quartz grains and sericite and much iron oxide.

The rock has been subjected to strong shearing force, producing a good example of schistose structure.

12--Quartzite--Same location as No. 9.

A compact rock of light red color, made up of uniformly rounded grains of quartz, and the feldspar with occasional grain of magnetite.

A fine siliceous material discolored by iron oxide, acts as a cement between the grains.

The quartz grains show secondary growth. 13--Altered Gabbro--Thirty-two Miles Above Wuchusk Nipi on Nascaupee River.

A coarse dark green rock whose principal constituents are pyroxene plagioclase and magnetite.

There is a slightly developed diabasic structure and the rock is much altered by weathering; the resultant product being chlorite.

14--Quartizite--Bibiquagin Lake.

Hard compact rock of light red color, cut in all directions by narrow veins of quartz, from microscope size to one-half an inch in width.

The grains of the constituent minerals, quartz, feldspar and magnetite have an angular brecciated appearance; showing uneven extinction and strong crushing effects.

The magnetite is somewhat decomposed, the resulting hematite filling the spaces between the quartz grains.

15--Anorthosite--Shore of Lake Michikamau.

A coarse grained rock of dark gray color, in which labradorite is the chief mineral. Magnetite and Kaolin are present in small quantities.

The labradorite contains inclusions of rutile and biotite and has a well-developed wedge structure and cross fracture due to the pressure and shearing which it has undergone.

It is also somewhat stained by the decomposition of the magnetite.

Sources of Information

On the map of the portage route to Lake Michikamau; that lake, the Grand River and Groswater Bay are taken from the map accompanying the report of Mr. A. P. Low.

The location of the Susan and Beaver Rivers with their tributaries was obtained from Dillon Wallace's map in "The Lure of the Labrador Wild."

The instruments used were a Brunton Pocket Transit, a small taffrail log and an Aneroid Barometer. Distances on land were approximated by means of a pedometer and by rough triangulation.

10160618R0

Made in the USA
Lexington, KY
29 June 2011